Yours is the
Kingdom

Yours is the Kingdom

A systematic theology of the Lord's Prayer

Gerald Bray

INTER-VARSITY PRESS
Norton Street, Nottingham NG7 3HR, England
Email: ivp@ivpbooks.com
Website: www.ivpbooks.com

First published 2007

British Library Cataloguing-in-Publication Data
A catalogue record for this book is available from the British Library.

ISBN: 978-1-84474-209-7

Set in Monotype Garamond 11/13pt
Typeset in Great Britain by Servis Filmsetting Ltd, Manchester
Printed and bound in Great Britain by Ashford Colour Press, Gosport,
Hampshire

*Inter-Varsity Press publishes Christian books that are true to the Bible and that communicate
the gospel, develop discipleship and strengthen the church for its mission in the world.*

*Inter-Varsity Press is closely linked with the Universities and Colleges Christian Fellowship, a
student movement connecting Christian Unions in universities and colleges throughout Great
Britain, and a member movement of the International Fellowship of Evangelical Students.
Website: www.uccf.org.uk*

CONTENTS

PREFACE

The Lord's Prayer is perhaps the best-known part of the Bible. Even in our supposedly 'post-Christian' world, it is still widely taught and learned, even by people who seldom enter a church. Those who remember the funeral of Diana, Princess of Wales, on 6 September 1997 may recall how the two million mourners who lined the route of the procession were asked to observe complete silence in her memory, and then to join together in reciting this prayer – and how many of that enormous number were able to do so without hesitation. It is true that modern-language Scriptures and forms of worship have created something of a generational divide, with older people knowing the traditional words and younger ones using more modern forms. However, the inconvenience of this is such that the familiar sixteenth-century version continues to be used, even in modern worship services – a unique survival that bears witness to the extent to which this prayer has become part of our common culture. It is even used in purely secular contexts, particularly by linguists, who have chosen it as their model text for comparing the features of one language with another. Its familiarity and universality appear to make it appropriate for this, as of course does its relative brevity.

Were the words as we know them ever intended to be used as a prayer? In Matthew's Gospel Jesus tells his followers to pray 'like this', which is somewhat ambiguous, though the parallel passage in Luke omits this qualification (Matt. 6:9; Luke 11:2). The snag is that virtually nobody has ever used Luke's shorter version in actual prayer! But by the end of the first century Christians were being advised to use Matthew's version at least three times a day (*Didache* 8.2), and it has always figured somewhere in virtually every form of publicly approved liturgy. In the 1662 Book of Common Prayer's service of Holy Communion it occurs twice, once at the beginning (without the doxology) and then again near the end with the doxology added, possibly because its note of praise and thanksgiving is an appropriate conclusion to the sacred feast.

In a recently published book on prayer, the late Huw Parri Owen devotes an entire chapter to the Lord's Prayer, which he, like so many others before him, saw as the 'pattern prayer' of the Christian church.[1] It has undoubtedly been the most widely used Christian prayer, but whether it has provided a model for other prayers is more debatable. There is no other liturgical prayer that can be said to reflect it in any significant way, and Christians who pray in their own words seldom if ever use it as a guide. It retains its prominence in the Christian consciousness, but it remains unique – unimitated and perhaps inimitable. How far it can be used as a pattern for our prayers is difficult to say. Of course its statements are unobjectionable enough, but most people would want to include far more than just these few lines in their own prayers, and other forms of prayer cannot be interpreted merely as a development or an elaboration of the Lord's Prayer. In short, though it is known and used in worship, it is not the source of our other prayers and if the church's liturgical tradition is any guide, nobody has ever thought that it should be.

Practically speaking, the Lord's Prayer is not a model for prayer in general, but if that is not what it is meant to be, what is its purpose? Surprising as it may seem, there has been very little serious reflection about this. Books on the Sermon on the Mount (which contains the Prayer) are fairly easy to come by and they obviously deal with the subject to some extent, but commentators tend to concentrate on the simplicity and straightforwardness of Jesus' approach to God and seldom venture much beyond that. That is an important emphasis, to be sure, but to a generation unfamiliar with the elaborate

---

1. H. P. Owen, *The Basis of Christian Prayer* (Vancouver: Regent College, 2006), pp. 79–106. The phrase occurs on p. 106.

rituals of Second Temple Judaism, the practical impact of this analysis is likely to be weak. Preachers and teachers can tell their people that they ought to be grateful to Jesus for having simplified our approach to God, but those who have never known anything else are liable to get the impression that relating to God is so simple that it hardly requires any thought at all. Those who attend modern services know how well that message has been communicated, and it may be somewhat paradoxical that in contemporary styles of worship the supposedly 'simple' words of the Lord's Prayer are seldom used, perhaps because many people think they sound formal and legalistic!

A new approach to the Lord's Prayer is required if it is to regain the place in our worship that its intrinsic merit and the universal tradition of the church suggest it ought to have. Many years ago I discovered that preaching on the Prayer, or parts of it, was a rewarding exercise, because its familiarity meant that even poorly taught congregations could follow along and deepen their spiritual understanding by relating to it. So when the invitation came to deliver the Moore College Lectures in Sydney in August 2006, and I was asked to choose a theme at once biblical, theological and pastoral, the Lord's Prayer immediately sprang to mind. A further invitation from the Latimer Fellowship of New Zealand enabled me to apply insights originally conceived for theological students to men and women engaged in parish ministry – an evolution from the laboratory to the workplace that sets the seal on the validity of anyone's theological reflections. Further thought and development have now doubled the length of the original lectures and turned them into the book you now hold in your hands.

As I have reflected more deeply on the Lord's Prayer I have become convinced that it is essentially an embryonic form of systematic theology. That theology is not expressed in the syllogisms and philosophical language of later ages; it is not even couched in the form of a creed! But the Prayer's structure and layout follow a clearly discernible pattern, beginning with God the Father who is the Creator Lord of heaven and earth, moving through the kingdom of his Son Jesus Christ to the blessings of both physical and spiritual nourishment which that brings, and concluding with the substance of the Christian life, which is the chief work of the Holy Spirit in our hearts. The Prayer does not cover every subject, but it is surprising how many vitally important matters are touched upon, once the deeper meaning of the text is sought. It is unnecessary to 'spiritualize' or allegorize Jesus' words in order to bring these out; most of the time, logical reflection is enough to make it clear what they are and it is left to us only to take the words into our souls and let them do their work of spiritual transformation within. It is my hope and prayer that the thoughts about the Lord's Prayer that I have put down in print will stir others to further reflection, so that together we may rediscover what a treasure we have in those words that are on the lips and in the hearts of all Christians.

It remains for me to thank the staff and students of Moore College for giving me the opportunity to develop my thinking about the Lord's Prayer, and to the clergy of the Church of Aotearoa New Zealand, in particular those of the dioceses of Christchurch, Dunedin and Waikato, who were exposed to it at an early stage and whose encouragement has been invaluable to me. I also owe an immense debt of gratitude to the congregation of St Paul's Church, Cambridge, to the Builders' Class of South Highland Presbyterian Church in Birmingham, Alabama, and especially to the faculty and students of Beeson Divinity School at Samford University in that city. It has been my privilege to spend fourteen happy years there and their prayers and support have undergirded the whole of this work, and much more besides. It is to all these brothers and sisters in the Lord that I dedicate this book, in the hope that it may be a small tribute to their faithfulness and ongoing witness to the power of prayer in the Christian life.

Gerald Bray

1. OUR FATHER IN HEAVEN, HALLOWED BE YOUR NAME

The text of the Lord's Prayer

No part of the Bible is more familiar to us than the few verses we know as the Lord's Prayer. It occurs twice in the Gospels, once in the Sermon on the Mount (Matt. 6:9–13) and again in Luke 11:2–4. Luke's text is noticeably shorter than Matthew's, but the latter contains everything found in Luke, and in virtually identical words. It is clear that the two texts must be related somehow, but determining that relationship is not a simple matter. New Testament scholars generally attribute material common to Matthew and Luke, but absent from Mark, to a source they usually refer to as Q.[1] Whether Q was ever a document in its own right is uncertain, and the Lord's Prayer is one of the more problematic texts attributed to it. On the one hand, the Greek is virtually identical in the two versions, which suggests that there was a standard translation of the original Aramaic, which may or may not have been transmitted

---

1. From the German word *Quelle*, which means 'source'.

in written form.[2] On the other hand, the context in which the Prayer is recorded is sufficiently different in the two Gospels to make it almost certain that one Evangelist was not copying the other, and unlikely that they were using a common source like the hypothetical Q. Most probably each was reflecting a different oral tradition, which had transmitted the same words of Jesus in two distinct forms. Is it possible to say that one of these is older or more 'authentic' than the other?

Most people think that Luke wrote his Gospel after Matthew, which, if true, would suggest the Matthaean version of the Prayer is older and more authentic. Certainly, it is the version that has gained general currency in the church, and the Lucan text has retreated so far into the background that it comes as a surprise to some people to discover it is there at all. But a closer reading of the two texts soon reveals that such an analysis is problematic. The Sermon on the Mount is a collection of Jesus' teachings, rather than a record of what he said on any occasion. Because of that, it does not help us much in determining what the circumstances were that gave rise to the Prayer. By contrast, the Lucan account tells us that it was originally a response to a request from the disciples for instruction as to how to pray, although we cannot tell at what point in his earthly ministry this request was made. The fact that the form of the prayer given in Luke is shorter and simpler than the one found in the Sermon on the Mount also leads us to suppose it to be more 'primitive' (and therefore presumably also more 'authentic') than the Matthaean version.

This impression is strengthened by the fact that the additions to the longer text are of a kind that balance the statements made in the shorter one and fill them out with phrases that appear to have

---

2. What the original Aramaic text was remains uncertain, although the Lord's Prayer (in its Matthaean form) was one of the few Gospel texts repeatedly translated back into that language. It is hard to believe that these so-called 'back translations' were entirely wide of the mark. But in the nature of the case, their reconstructions must remain hypothetical, so they can be used only with caution as evidence for interpreting the meaning of the text.

been taken from Jewish liturgical sources. It is therefore tempting to conclude that the Lucan version goes back to Jesus himself and that the Matthaean one represents a later redaction designed to make the prayer usable in Christian worship. That may have been the case, but we must be cautious about rejecting the authenticity of the longer version. It is not impossible that it also comes from Jesus, since he must have given the same basic teaching on many different occasions and would presumably have seen no reason not to adapt his words to fit the circumstances. We have to remember that only the Matthaean version has been used consistently in Christian worship, and that it is found as early as the *Didache*, which repeats it virtually word for word (*Didache* 8.2).[3] Matthew's version was therefore certainly in existence at a time when eyewitnesses to the teaching of Jesus were still alive, and as it is generally agreed that he was particularly sensitive to the Jewish and Palestinian background of Jesus' ministry it is perfectly possible that the Prayer reflects that. Furthermore, Matthew's additions complement and round out what is found in Luke, whose text seems too brusque to have formed a prayer on its own. Luke's version tells us what should be in our prayers, but does not really stand as a prayer in its own right.

Perhaps that is the answer. Jesus may have taught his disciples the principles of prayer (Luke) and then turned them into a prayer for use by a wider public (Matthew). In the first instance, Jesus was responding to a request from the disciples, who had been impressed by the way in which John the Baptist had taught his followers to pray. In the second, he was attacking the hypocritical prayers of the Pharisees, who were more interested in impressing their fellow Jews than in communicating with God. In that

---

3. There are very minor differences between this version and Matthew's and they can almost all be attributed to editorial corrections designed to make the Greek more grammatically acceptable. The only real difference is that the *Didache* adds the final doxology (though without mentioning the kingdom). See the concluding chapter for a discussion of this. The date of the *Didache* is uncertain, but it may have been as early as AD 55 and is probably not later than AD 110.

context, it would have been natural for Jesus to have provided his hearers with an actual prayer, modelled on those they were already familiar with, and there is no reason to suppose he did not do so. Like Matthew, the *Didache* also makes it clear that Jesus was responding to the behaviour of hypocrites, though it does not specify who these hypocrites were. We are therefore perfectly justified in concluding that both forms of the prayer go back to Jesus himself, and that the differences between them are most likely the product of particular circumstances rather than the work of some later redactor. But even if the precise wording of the longer version was left to his disciples, there can be no doubt that the version we now recognize as the Lord's Prayer reflects the essential teaching of Jesus and goes back to the very beginnings of the Christian church.

Modern minds may find it puzzling that Jesus' disciples would have asked him to teach them how to pray. Nowadays, most people simply close their eyes and say whatever comes into their minds when they want to pray, and do not think of asking anybody how they should do it. We regard prayer as the spontaneous outpouring of the heart, and it seems odd to us that it should have to be learned as a set form of words. To our minds, using someone else's words as a vehicle for prayer seems inauthentic and even somewhat hypocritical, and it is surprising to find Jesus giving his disciples a fixed form to use. We may even be inclined to suggest that he was merely laying down general principles for prayer, and did not expect his disciples to use his exact words themselves.

In ancient times, however, spontaneous prayer was not at all the normal pattern. The disciples of Jesus would not have been used to praying in their own words, improvising as they went along. To them, prayer was something that had to be learned, and this is why they asked Jesus to teach them how to pray. In their experience, prayer was a formal, liturgical event, conducted by the priests in the temple or by the rabbis in the synagogue. These patterns of formal prayer are well known, and scholars have shown how influential they were in the early church. This would hardly have been the case if the disciples had not accepted their Jewish inheritance as the norm for public worship. Furthermore, the prayers in a Galilean synagogue would have been in Hebrew, which was fast becoming a dead language in Jesus' day – although Aramaic-speaking people would readily have understood much of it. If the prayers were in an archaic form of language, they would almost certainly have been ritualized to a considerable extent – couched in set phrases that those who led public worship would have memorized as part of their training, since the language did not come naturally to those who were required to use it. The prayers would therefore have had a carefully worked out structure, beginning with the praise and adoration of God and continuing with thanksgiving for his blessings, contrition for the sins of the people and supplication for mercy, forgiveness and blessing. Not all of these ingredients would have been present in equal measure in every prayer, but some combination of them would have been found in most forms of public worship.

Perhaps the disciples of Jesus also realized that the character of his teaching would be revealed in what he had to say about prayer, since it is in prayer that the worshipper comes closest to God. Prayer is our communication with him, a communication framed in human speech, but human speech aided by spiritual power from above. As the apostle Paul said to the Roman church some time later, the Holy Spirit prays for us when our words are inadequate, as they must always be when we have a direct encounter with Almighty God (cf. Rom. 8:26). But to say that our words are inadequate to express the depth of our relationship with God does not mean they are completely useless for that purpose. As the utterances of finite beings limited by the constraints of space and time, words are bound to be inadequate to address an infinite God who sees and knows things in ways impossible for us. But God has thrown us a lifeline, given us an instruction manual you might say, which teaches us how we can use words to communicate with him and talk about him in spite of our human finitude. Certain words have been invested with special meanings designed to lift us above and beyond our creaturely limitations and give us a foretaste of God himself. These words are valid for those who have faith, as nearly two thousand years of church history have demonstrated. To those who do not, they stand as a witness to what Christians believe to be true, namely that there is a God above who cares about us enough to have sent his Son into the world to save us from our sins and to open the gate of heaven, so that we may rise and spend eternity with him. When we get there, we shall have no further need of 'prayer' as we understand that now, because our entire life will be one of prayer and praise to God in the fullness of his eternal being.

Prayer is what theologians call a 'means of grace' – a way of entering the life of God but which is something less than that the fullness of that life itself. It is a means to an end, not the end itself, but it should not be ignored or undervalued, because it is the means laid down by God for attaining the end he has appointed for us. To pray is to draw closer to God; to do it in the way he has taught us is to come closer in the way he has prescribed for us, and is therefore an assurance that we are heading in the right direction.

It is because prayer is a guide into experiencing the eternal reality of God that it is theological, and it is for this reason that the most effective prayer will also be the truest theology. Liturgists like to use a Latin phrase, *lex orandi lex credendi*, by which they mean that the way we pray determines the content of what we believe, but I would suggest that it is really the other way round. It is what we believe that determines the way we pray, because unless we have the end firmly in our sights, the means will not help us to get there. A car is a means to an end, but if we do not know where we are going in it, it is useless and potentially dangerous. Prayer is the spiritual vehicle that leads us into the presence of God, but unless it is handled in the right way it may take us in altogether the wrong direction and lead us badly astray. Just as cars are of varying worth, so prayers can be of vastly different quality, and we want only the best to take us safely to our destination. The disciples of Jesus sensed this, and before setting out on their spiritual journey they wisely asked the expert what vehicle they ought to use to get them there. What Jesus offered them for their pilgrimage was what we now call the Lord's Prayer – the surest and safest guide to the heavenly kingdom; that kingdom he has promised us as the inheritance of those who have been called, who have been set apart and who are now being prepared to reign with him in eternity.

The Lord's Prayer is not a mantra, intended to be repeated mindlessly over and over again as a kind of ritual chant. It is rather a form of teaching, a pattern to be followed and adapted intelligently to different situations and varying needs. It is simple, but its simplicity conceals great depth, which it is the privilege of the expositor to attempt to fathom. No part of the New Testament has been commented on by more people over a longer period of time than this Prayer, and no part of the Bible sums up more concisely what it really means to know God and to serve him as we ought. Already around the year AD 200, Tertullian had written a commentary on it, making it the first part of the New Testament to have been expounded in this way. Later it became the standard source for teaching Christians the meaning of prayer, and in the Middle Ages it was singled out as one of the set texts for those seeking ordination into the church's ministry.[4] That status ensured it would be studied and commented upon for centuries, and by the time of the Reformation it formed part of a trilogy that included the Apostles' Creed (doctrine) and the Ten Commandments (discipline). The Lord's Prayer was the crowning glory, because it taught devotion, the ultimate goal for which the other two were merely a preparation. Even as late as the seventeenth century, we still find the Puritan writer Thomas Watson (d. 1686) following the same pattern. Watson replaced the Apostles' Creed with the Westminster Confession of Faith, but otherwise he stuck to the ancient model and his book *The Lord's Prayer* is still a classic work on the subject today.[5]

Above all, the Lord's Prayer is a theological text, because it teaches us about God, and teaching about God is what we call 'theology'. Moreover, the Lord's Prayer does this in a coherent way, and so its teaching must be described as systematic. Because of that, we can say that it is the earliest expression of systematic theology we have, and we know that, in substance at least, it comes from the lips of Jesus himself. This means that Jesus taught his

---

4. Evidence for this can be found in the statutes of Bishop Peter Quivel of Exeter, which date from about 1287. It is clear, however, that the bishop was simply restating already established practice.

5. It originally appeared as part of his *A Body of Divinity*, first published in 1691, but is now available as a separate volume.

disciples to think about God and to speak to him in a way that makes sense, even if the Prayer's logic is not always that of the world around us. Most importantly, the notion that our doctrine is one thing and our devotion something quite different is refuted by the Lord's Prayer, which not only combines the two but also anchors its devotion in its doctrine. As we proceed to unlock the doors to the knowledge of God that each word and phrase represents, we shall see for ourselves what treasures lie within, and come to appreciate how each new line takes us one step further towards the courts of the heavenly kingdom, our spiritual destination to which the Lord's Prayer remains a supreme and infallible guide.

Our Father

When you pray, say, 'Our Father'. Nothing is more important in prayer than the person to whom the prayer is directed. In the ancient world, there were many gods, and it was quite possible to address some of them, at least, as 'father'. The most obvious example of this is the Roman god Jupiter, whose name is simply a combination of the words 'Jove' and 'father' – *Iovis pater* as it would have been in Old Latin. In the Acts of the Apostles, Paul mentions the fact that there were pagan poets who acknowledged the supreme being as their father, if only in a roundabout way, by calling themselves his 'offspring' (Acts 17:28), and he used this to show the pagans of Athens that they were closer to the God of Israel than they might have imagined. The curious thing is that although Israel could also have thought in such terms, since the Old Testament speaks of Israel as God's 'inheritance' (Ps. 78:71), a word that at least suggests a father–son relationship, it did not do so. Old Testament allusions to the fatherhood of God are rare and vague. Far more common and more explicit is the term 'servant', which is often used to describe the relationship of Israel to God, and which was picked up and used to such effect by the apostle Paul, who told the first Christians that they were no longer servants, but had become children of God by adoption (Gal. 4:1–7).

The New Testament evidence suggests that the Israelites did not address God as Father because the use of such a word implied a kind of relationship to God that they could not accept. In their eyes, to be a child of God, as opposed to a servant, was to share the nature of God, and that was impossible. As a being in his own right, God was totally different from his creation and from any of his creatures, including humans, in spite of the fact that Adam and Eve were created in his image (Gen. 1:26–27). When Jesus called God his Father, pious Jews were scandalized, because in their eyes, he was making himself equal with God (John 5:18). For Jesus to teach his disciples to pray to God as their Father was therefore highly daring in the Jewish context. He may have appeared to be introducing some form of paganism; worse, he was suggesting to his followers that they shared God's nature in some undefined but clearly unacceptable way. Neither alternative was very appealing to the Jewish leaders of his day, and the form of worship he was proposing was generally regarded as incompatible with contemporary Jewish understandings of Israel's relationship to God. It is clear that those who prayed 'Our Father' were moving on to something else – to a new perception of God that did not come naturally to Jews and, as taught by Jesus, came across as something fundamentally new and disturbing.

Of course, it can always be said that 'Father' may be equivalent to 'Creator', and no-one could have objected to referring to God as that. But although this is theoretically true, it does not reflect the biblical usage of either term. The relationship Jesus had with his Father was far more intimate than one he would have had with a mere creator. After all, everyone on earth, and even Satan and his angels, could legitimately call God their Creator, but the forces of evil would never have referred to him as their Father. Jesus himself revealed this, if only indirectly, when he told the Pharisees that their father was the devil, because in spiritual terms they were much closer to him than they were to Abraham, let alone to Abraham's God, whom they professed to worship (John 8:44). The use of the word 'father' implies a spiritual affinity that goes well beyond the physical relationship, and it is this aspect that is fundamentally new in Jesus' teaching.

Having said this, we must also remember that ancient Israel had a special relationship with God, and that there were great saints in the Old Testament who communed with him in the most intimate way. Yet, however close they were to God, the nature of their relationship to him was still one of master and servant, not of father and son. The spiritual kinship that existed between God and his people was established by law and maintained by obedience to that law. It was Israel's inability to fulfil its obligations that caused the spiritual crisis the New Testament sought to address. The means for having fellowship with God were available, but the people could not make proper use of them because the nature and effects of their sin were too great. So problematic was this that the Pharisees had reinterpreted the law in a way that made it possible for them to keep it. They had reduced great spiritual principles of universal application to petty rules that were often troublesome and inconvenient to keep, but which could be managed by those who had the time, resources and dedication to do so. Others were less fortunate and almost bound to fall short somehow or other, but that merely justified the spiritual elite's propensity for feeling superior not only to Gentiles but to fellow Jews. Time and again, Jesus pointed out the hypocrisy of this attitude, which had turned a reverent and pious servanthood into an ungodly slavery. He preached that only by going in the opposite direction – by raising the servants to the status of sons – could this problem be tackled and solved, and that that was what he had come to do.

In teaching his disciples to pray 'Our Father', Jesus was inducting them into his own relationship with God. But what kind of relationship was that, and to what extent was it possible for his disciples to share in it? As we have already said, by calling God his Father, Jesus was thought to be making himself equal with God, a charge he never denied and which his actions tended to confirm. Whoever we are, we share with our human fathers something far more than a general affinity. Frequently, we may look like them, think like them and act like them. In some mysterious way, we embody them in the next generation in ways often subconscious but easily spotted by those who have known our fathers as well as ourselves. For Jesus to claim God as his Father was to claim all this for himself – and more. As a human being, I reflect certain characteristics of my human father to varying degrees, but these are relative because neither I nor my father have any particular characteristic to an absolute degree. For example, we may both have a good sense of humour, but probably not an identical one, and there will almost certainly be any number of differences of detail between his and mine. Even if these differences are small ones and hard for outsiders to perceive, they can cause difficulties in father–son relationships because fathers sometimes find it hard to understand why their sons are not exactly like themselves!

In the case of Jesus, to be like his Father means to be like someone absolute and who therefore possesses all his attributes to an absolute degree. God the Father cannot be more or less than what he is, and so anyone who is like him must be exactly the same as him. You cannot be like an absolute without being an absolute yourself, because that is what being an absolute is all about. For this reason, Jesus could not have been like his Father without being the same as he is, and if that is the case, then Jesus must also have been God. To put it differently, just as the natural son of a human father is also human, so the natural son of a divine Father must also be divine. And because there is only one God, his natural Son cannot be divine without being identical with him. The problem then becomes one of working out how Jesus can be identical to the Father and still remain a distinct person in his own right. It is this question that gave rise to the Christian doctrine of the Trinity. After trying many different possibilities, the church eventually decided that the best solution was to describe God as three Persons (Father, Son and Holy Spirit) who coexist in one divine nature. The Persons are exactly like each other in their divine being, but are distinguishable by a distinct identity revealed in their mutual relationships. This makes them equal but different, so that when Jesus prays to his Father, he is praying to another Person, but he can claim the right to be heard because he is that Person's equal.

To put it differently, when we ask *what* God is, we answer that he is invisible, eternal, holy and so on, and these descriptions of him apply equally to all three Persons. But when we ask *who* God is, we have to say that he is a Trinity of Persons bound to each other by the love they share. Because all three are infinite and equally divine, you cannot know one of the Persons without knowing the other two as well. This helps to explain why, when Jesus told his disciples who he was and what he had come to do, he almost always defined himself in relation to his Father, the one who had sent him. When he talked about the Holy Spirit, it was as the 'other Comforter' who would replace him and do even greater things than he had done – a sure sign that Jesus thought of him as his equal and therefore as the Father's equal also (John 16:4–15).

As Christians, we believe that Jesus is 'God from God, Light from Light, true God from true God', as the words of the Nicene Creed put it.[6] But how does this carry over into our relationship with God? How can God be our Father, when we are clearly not in the same exalted position as Jesus is? Jesus' relationship to his heavenly Father is one of absolute identity, but ours can only be relative, because we are not divine. If we as creatures are fundamentally different from God our Creator, what does it mean for us to call him our Father? The New Testament solves this problem by saying that although we are not children of God by nature, as Jesus was, we have been adopted as his children by grace. This means that whereas Jesus was eternally begotten of the Father, we have been chosen by God at a particular moment in time and integrated into his family. We have no natural resemblance to God, and therefore have no claim on his attention, but because God loved us, he decided to reach out and bring us into fellowship with him. This action, which we have neither asked for nor done anything to deserve, is what we ascribe to his 'grace', and it leads to eternal life with the Persons of the Trinity in heaven.

How appropriate is it for us to use the word 'Father' to describe our relationship with God? Earlier generations did not have a problem with this. Jesus had taught his disciples to pray that way, and that was good enough for them. More recently, two factors have emerged that have called this ancient tradition into question. The first may broadly be described as 'feminism'. Why do we call God 'Father' and not 'Mother'? Is this terminology fixed, or does it simply reflect sexist attitudes (or what some social analysts like to call 'patriarchy') standard in biblical times but now abandoned? The other issue, which may or may not be linked to this, concerns the problematic understanding of fatherhood so prevalent today.

---

6. The Nicene Creed is named after the first council of Nicaea, held there in AD 325, but in fact it probably comes from a later council, held at Constantinople in AD 381.

At a time when many families have broken up and a good many fathers have rejected their responsibilities to their children, is this image really the best one for us to use now? Should we feel free to adapt biblical usage to modern times, and if so, how free should we be?

On the first question, we have to say that although God is not a sexual being in the human sense, he has revealed himself to us as 'masculine'. Very occasionally there are hints of a feminine touch in God's dealings with his people, but this never reaches the point of accepting the use of female imagery for God as a general principle.[7] Why not? One possible explanation is that the ancient world was full of fertility cults, which often involved temple prostitution with priestesses of the goddess. Israel rejected that kind of thing completely and if it was true that feminine language about God was liable to lead to that kind of interpretation, then it obviously had to be avoided. That explanation is possible, but we must remember that there were also a large number of male fertility gods in the pagan pantheon and Israel rejected them too. Furthermore, there is no suggestion in the Bible itself that fear of such contamination played any role in determining the way in which God revealed himself to his people.

The true explanation of this has to be sought from within the logic of the biblical revelation itself. If God had revealed himself as a Mother–Daughter combination, how would the incarnation of the Daughter have been possible? She could not have entered the womb of the Virgin Mary, since then not only would she have had two mothers – one divine, and the other human – but there would have been no room for the male principle at all. It is therefore much easier to imagine the incarnation of a divine Son in the womb of a human mother than it is to imagine the incarnation of a divine daughter. The incarnation of a male avoids the unnecessary reduplication of having two mothers and permits both sexes to play a part in the coming of the Saviour. Of course, as a matter of historical fact, nobody doubts that Jesus Christ was a male, so the Father–Son imagery imposes itself more or less automatically.

---

7. Cf. Matt. 23:37 for an example of this.

The feminine principle is also invoked, but it is with reference to the church, which is the 'bride of Christ' (Rev. 21:9). In that respect, we can say that every believer is 'female' in relation to Christ, an important point to remember when accusations of 'patriarchy' are raised. Paradoxical as it may seem, it is because we are *sons* of God that he has sent the Spirit of his Son into our hearts, crying 'Abba, Father' (Gal. 4:6), but it is as his *bride* that we shall sit at the great wedding feast of the Lamb when the end of all things finally comes. In the language used of believers, the metaphorical aspects of human sexuality are exploited to the full and the male–female divide is transcended. Nevertheless, although we can shift from one sex to the other in our relationship to him, he remains the same – our Father, not our Mother.

The question raised by the existence of deadbeat fathers, particularly in the modern Western world, is a rather different one. The fact that some people, perhaps even a great many people, have problematic relationships with their human fathers does not by itself invalidate the biblical imagery. God is not to be regarded as a heavenly projection of our earthly fathers and judged accordingly. On the contrary, if there is any connection at all between these two things, it must surely be that God our heavenly Father speaks to our human deficiencies in this respect, as in others, and supplies what is missing in them. Beaten and abandoned by an earthly parent we may be, but if that happens we can be sure that God will enfold us in his everlasting arms and comfort us in ways no human being can match. No physical father, however good and responsible, can ever take the place of God. Even the best are but pale imitations of him. It is true that many people find it difficult to relate to their human fathers, who often appear to be more remote and less emotional than their mothers. But if a mother's love for her children is instinctive (cf. Isa. 49:15), a father's love is likely to be more rational and 'purpose-driven', to use a popular modern phrase. Typically, it is the mother who nurses children through their early years, but as they grow older, the father assumes more responsibility in preparing them for adulthood. This is what our heavenly Father does for us. He does not love us because we are an extension of himself (which we are not) but because he has created us so that we might dwell for ever in eternity with him. To achieve this has cost him a great deal. 'God so loved the world', said John, 'that he gave his only Son, that whoever believes in him should not perish but have eternal life' (John 3:16). That is the Father's love at work, and in praying to him as our Father, we appropriate that love and claim its protection and power for our own lives.

Being adopted by God

But why does God love us and want us to live with him eternity, when we have turned away from him and have done nothing to deserve this? The reason is that he originally created us in his image, with the intention that we should live with him for ever. The image of God in us is best understood as our personhood, that is to say, our ability to create and sustain relationships with other persons, whether they are human or divine. As human beings we have an inbuilt relationship with God, which nothing can change or diminish. Even when we disobey his will, the image of God is still present in us to remind us that we have a relationship with him that we have rejected by our foolish behaviour. We are responsible for this, which is why the first step on the road to recovery is a recognition that we are guilty because of what we have done. Unless we get to that point, our relationship with God cannot be restored because we shall have failed to understand what it is all about. If I go to the dentist to have a tooth filled and he puts a filling in without cleaning out the cavity first, that filling will not do me any good. It is the same with our relationship to God. The 'bad news' of our guilt is not meant to put us off, but to show us what has to be cleaned out before his new life can be filled in. I do not like it when my dentist tells me the truth and I feel ashamed for not having followed his advice before it was too late, but I am grateful to him for telling me what needs to be done and for getting on with it. I certainly do not want him to pretend that everything is just fine as it is! It is the same with God. People who think it unpleasant to be told they are 'miserable sinners', who are lost and without God in the world, are right in a way – it most certainly is not pleasant! But it is the truth, and God tells us the truth, not to crush us but to restore us and to make us the people he wants us to be. He is our Creator and he is also our Judge, to be sure, but above all, he is our Father, whose creative acts and judgments are all heading in the same direction – rescuing us and making us fit to live with him in heaven.

As human persons, we have an inbuilt relationship with God but share none of his attributes – unlike him, we are not omniscient, omnipotent, omnipresent, invisible, impassible or immortal. To the very limited extent that we can participate in any of these characteristics, it is only because God dwells in us by his Holy Spirit, allowing us to benefit from things we do not ourselves possess. Even then, there is a very limited range of divine attributes in which we can truly share – holiness and immortality being the most important of them. We may be given unusual wisdom, but not omniscience, just as we may be granted extraordinary strength to endure suffering, but not impassibility. Even in the case of the so-called 'communicable attributes' of God, the ones he is said to be able to share with us, it is highly questionable as to whether he really does so. God calls me to be holy, but can I possess a holiness distinct from his presence in my life? Can I be so filled with the Holy Spirit of God that my sinfulness will be removed and my created human nature be changed into something else? This will happen after death, as we are told in 1 Corinthians 15:35–55, but is it possible in this life?

Some have held that it is, and even spiritual giants like John Wesley have been known to fall into this trap, which theologians call 'perfectionism'. But the paradoxical truth of the matter is that the holier people become, the more they are aware of their own innate sinfulness, which (in objective terms) is the very opposite of holiness. This is because the light of God's presence in our lives illuminates the darkness and makes us see more clearly just how dark it really is. Hard as it is to fathom, I am closest to God when I realize how unlike him I really am! When we consider the question of immortality, we should remember that the apostle Paul said, 'And the life I now live in the flesh I live by faith in the Son of God, who loved me and gave himself for me' (Gal. 2:20). On this analysis, the new spiritual life I have as a child of God is not really mine but Christ's. It has been given to me as an act of love on his part, but it remains essentially his, not mine. Stop and think about it for a moment and you will realize that this has to be so, because if my spiritual life really belonged to me, it would be relative and imperfect – even if it was somehow free from sin. A righteousness of that kind might restore my life on earth by putting me back into the state of Adam and Eve before they fell, but it would not get me to heaven any more than it got them there. Only Christ's life can do that, because only his life is heavenly to begin with. When we call God our Father, we do so because Christ has allowed us to appropriate his Sonship for that purpose. 'It is no longer I who live, but Christ who lives in me' (Gal. 5:20). That, not anything I do or can do, is the hope of glory for me.

So to pray 'Our Father' is first of all to confess that Jesus has the right to pray to God in this way because God is his natural Father, whereas for us it is a privilege he has graciously allowed us to share. This is because we have been united to Christ by the power of his Holy Spirit, who enables us to pray in this way both legitimately and effectively – legitimately because we have been adopted by Christ, and effectively because, thanks to our adoption, God has put his Holy Spirit in our hearts. To pray 'Our Father' is to know all three Persons of the Trinity, because only in and through the Trinity is such prayer possible. To pray 'Our Father' is to enter a new relationship with God, one rooted in his inner being, which gives us access to his mind in a way that would not otherwise happen. To be a servant or, as we would say today, an employee, is certainly no disgrace. There are many examples of perfectly respectable master–servant or employer–employee relationships, and when these work well, great loyalty and affection can be generated on both sides. But at the end of the day that relationship is a limited one, determined by contract and governed by law. The value of an employee is measured by his or her ability to fulfil the terms of this arrange-ment, and if this does not work, it will be terminated. The essential difference between this and a family relationship is well understood by the world around us, and in most workplaces, close relatives are not allowed to work together for precisely this reason. A good employer–employee relationship depends on maintaining a certain distance between the parties, and if it gets entangled in a family situation, it may be seriously compromised and unable to function as it should.

By moving our relationship with God from the level of master–servant to that of the family, Jesus changed everything. The relationship he has given us with the Father is not a contractual obligation determined by law, but a unity of thought and purpose governed by love. It is true, of course, that there are common elements between servanthood and sonship – most notably the obligation to obey what the Father tells us to do, but even these work out somewhat differently in practice. The obedience of an employee is contractual and carries no personal responsibility with it. For example, a secretary types the boss's letters without questioning their content, and is not held responsible for what they say. He or she may be called upon to explain the boss's intentions to an enquirer, but if unable to do this satisfactorily, will not be blamed for keeping a confidence or confessing ignorance – quite the reverse in fact! It is very different with children who are taken on as partners and destined to inherit the firm. Children are called to obey their parents, but they have a way of being inquisitive about this, and wise parents will do their best to explain what is expected of them and why. It even happens that parents sometimes change their minds, develop new ideas or accede to a child's wishes in the course of this process, without losing their fundamental authority. On the contrary, the willingness of parents to listen often increases the respect children have for them (because they are being taken seriously), and even if the outcome is not what the child originally wanted, the relationship itself may be strengthened and deepened as a result of this dialogue and consultation.

In theological language, this process is called 'intercessory prayer', the privilege given to us as children of God to question our Father's will and ask him to listen to our point of view. He always does so, but his response will vary according to the nature of the request. Sometimes, he will grant it because it is fundamentally in accordance with his will, whether we realize this or not. Sometimes, he will grant it because he knows that although it is wrong for us, we shall only learn our lesson the hard way. That was the case in ancient Israel, when the people pleaded for a king and

God granted their petition – but only after warning them what the consequences would be (1 Sam. 8:10–22). At other times he says no, either because the time is not right or because he has another plan for us, which we cannot yet see or understand. When this happens, we react the way children do – sometimes happily, sometimes angrily, sometimes with a blank expression which shows that we have not understood the message. But however we respond to our Father, he still loves us, still wants us and still goes on taking care of us, even if we do not appreciate it at the time. We belong to him, after all, and whatever we may think, say or do, he is not going to let us go.

This is how God treats his adopted sons and daughters. He continues to be responsible for our welfare and always has our best interests close to his heart. His plan for us is carefully worked out so that we will derive the maximum benefit from it, even if there are times when it appears to us to be otherwise. As we grow, we are faced with new challenges and forced to accept greater responsibilities appropriate to our age and experience. Sometimes this involves adaptations and compromises that are painful, particularly if we are not ready and prepared to accept them. A child may find potty training uncongenial and resist it, even to the point of forcefully rejecting it at first, but no sensible parent would let the child get away with this indefinitely, since an untrained adult would be an unbearable anomaly. We may not remember how we overcame this hurdle in our own lives, but we can certainly look back on it and be grateful that our parents persisted in spite of whatever objections we might have made at the time! As the process of maturing becomes more conscious, it may also become harder to accept. How many children instinctively believe that parents are twenty-four-hour cash machines with unlimited drawing rights attached, only to discover to their discomfort that a day comes when the card runs out and the newly formed adult has to make his or her own way in the world! And let us not even begin to think about the strong-willed, independently minded pensioner who has always lived independently and then at the age of ninety-three is told she must stop driving, move into sheltered accommodation and let somebody else take responsibility for the things she can no longer do on her own. We do not even have to wait that long – try

telling a forty-year-old man that he can no longer play football the
way he used to, especially if he has not done it for twenty years,
and see how far you get! Many a middle-aged man lands up in a
cast or worse, simply because he cannot accept his own limitations
and insists, against all evidence to the contrary, that he is the
master of his own destiny. Will we ever learn?

So it is in our relationship with our heavenly Father. The
employer–employee relationship is basically fixed, though it may
be altered by promotions from time to time. But the Father–son
relationship is organic and in a constant state of growth and
fluctuation. Human parents sometimes find this hard to accept
and may have to be reminded that the baby they used to push in
the pram is now driving the family car, but this is mainly because
adults find that time creeps up on them unawares, not because
they ever expected their offspring to remain perpetually adoles-
cent. Our heavenly Father actively encourages us to grow up, and
much of the New Testament is devoted to helping us achieve that
purpose. We are constantly being urged to go on to higher things,
to become 'perfect' as the Bible puts it, in our faith and behaviour
(Col. 1:28). This 'perfection' is not some abstract notion of total
infallibility but a call to maturity, so that we shall act and react in
ways that correspond to the depth and strength of the life we have
in God our Father. For that to happen, we have to be sorted out,
and this will almost invariably be painful in one way or another.
It is all too easy for us to get fixed in our ways, rooted in a particular routine and impervious to the call of God to move on to
greater things.

The teenage years are especially hard, because then spiritual
development is often out of harmony with self-awareness and
readiness to accept new challenges and responsibilities. We may be
too eager for these and end up falling flat on our faces, or else too
reluctant – appearing to others to be stronger and more capable
than we imagine ourselves to be. Fifteen-year-olds can go either
way, sometimes even both ways at once, and parents hardly know
what to do with them much of the time. To make things even
more difficult, teenagers have a mixed relationship with their
parents – deeply dependent on them in one sense and longing for
their approval, but also struggling to be free and mortified if the

older generation steps in when and where it is not wanted! The painful truth we have to face here is that the church is full of spiritual teenagers, who have this on-off relationship to God. But tedious as this can often be, it is still better than slavery. A slave will never change, but a teenager will eventually grow up and look back on those years with a mixture of shame and relief – shame that he or she ever behaved like that, and relief that the consequences of such foolishness turned out to be less serious than they could have been.

This is how God deals with us. When we let him down, as we invariably do, he does not send us packing, but draws us closer to himself, shows us why it matters to him that we should change our ways and then sends us off with renewed assurance and encouragement. When we crash the family car, blow our money in reckless behaviour, waste the best years of our lives in the wrong company and ruin every chance we ever had in life, it is likely to be our parents who step in to pay our debts, restore us to civilized society and equip us to go on to new and far greater things. So it is with God. In the famous story of the prodigal son the older brother, who may have represented the Jewish people, was resentful and stand-offish at this treatment of the undeserving younger son, but in real life it is our older brother, the Lord Jesus Christ, who came to earth to pay the price demanded for our wrongdoing and to reconcile us to God. We are 'family' in God's eyes, and when the chips were down, it was the family which came to our rescue in the person of the firstborn and only natural Son, whose sacrificial death is the key and foundation stone of our eternal life.

Finally, as our Father, God provides for our eternal destiny. Good parents lay up stores for their children, plan for their future and make great sacrifices so that their children will have the best they can afford to give. What our human parents do with great effort but achieve only to a relative degree, since not even the richest of them can provide us with everything, God does out of the fullness of his heart and resources. The inheritance he has laid up for us is neither finite nor perishable – it is boundless and eternal in its scope and duration. It is not something to be measured in possessions or monetary wealth, but something far greater than these. It is in effect a share in the ruling of his kingdom, the ultimate degree of union and communion it is possible for us to have with him. When we enter his presence it is not as pensioners or as extras hidden away in the corner of some huge family photograph, but as kings seated alongside him on his throne of glory, ready and able to judge the world and even the angels (1 Cor. 6:3). Just as Queen Elizabeth carries no money, because all the coin of the realm is hers, so we shall have no need of things to call our own, because once we get to heaven, everything there will be ours! This is why the reward for the children is the same regardless of their age. In the parable of the labourers in the vineyard, those who come in at the eleventh hour will have exactly the same reward as those who have worked all day (Matt. 20:1–16). It may even be that they too will have to wait until all of us have been safely gathered in, as the saints of the Old Testament most certainly had to do (Heb. 11:39–40). This may seem unfair in human terms, but in the context of heaven, where all God's children are treated equally, no other solution is possible. God is no respecter of persons. In his presence the distinctions and claims that matter so much to us here on earth will vanish as we are gathered round his eternal throne, united in his family and given the inheritance of the children we have been made, not by nature but by the grace of adoption in Jesus Christ.

In heaven

We have spent a long time considering what it means to call God 'Our Father', but it has been time well spent, because everything about our relationship with God is determined by its fundamental nature. Now it is time to move on to what Jesus tells us about the Father in the very next line – he dwells in heaven. The assumption is that heaven is somewhere other than where we are right now.[8] We shall look into this in detail later, but for the moment let us consider what this means for our Father and for the relationship we have with him. The first

---

8. This detail is not in the Lucan version, but in substance it undoubtedly reflects the teaching of Jesus, who often spoke to his disciples about their 'heavenly Father'.

thing that must be said is that the word 'heaven' in the Bible carries a double meaning, or at least it has a double point of reference. On the one hand, heaven is a physical place, created by God 'in the beginning' and populated by the sun, the moon and the stars. On the other hand, it is also a spiritual state, inhabited by angels, archangels and all the heavenly hosts, including (we are told) the spirits of those who have been redeemed from the earth (cf. Rev. 14:1–5). The two dimensions of heaven are closely connected, not in physical terms but in mental association. The physical universe has been given to us as a reminder of our own finitude and insignificance in the bigger scheme of things, as the Bible often reminds us. When Job questioned his fate, God pointed the universe out to him, and put Job's complaints into their proper perspective (Job 38). As the heavens are higher than the earth, wrote Isaiah, so are God's thoughts higher than our thoughts, and his ways higher than our ways (Isa. 55:9). The message is plain, and how much anguish and bitterness would be avoided if only we could bring ourselves to accept it and apply it in our lives.

The heavens are higher than we are and out of our reach, but they are visible to us and we can know them in some depth and detail. So it is with God also. We can never hope to encompass him in our thoughts, still less bring him under our control. We shall no more have a first-hand, sensory perception of him than we shall wander through distant galaxies touching down on strange planets. This will not stop human minds from trying to do this, of course, and the existence of outer space is the perfect invitation to speculation. The *Star Trek* mentality is alive and well in our society, and science fiction writers have a wonderful time inventing distant worlds in which strangely humanoid creatures live fantastic lives in technological terms, but lives punctured by the same cosmic struggle between good and evil that we know here on earth. Indeed, it sometimes seems that the further away our imagination gets, the starker this conflict becomes, and that whole solar systems are in the grip of one evil empire or another. The ancients were much the same as we are in this respect. It is true that they were more inclined to put their imaginary kingdoms under the sea or on the far sides of the earth – inventing the Antipodes, for example, long before they were actually discovered. But they shared the belief that the heavens were populated with superhuman beings whose capacities far outpaced ours but whose moral depravity was very similar, or even worse. The common thread that unites ancient and modern speculations of this kind is the feeling that out there is something greater than ourselves, whether good or bad, and that somehow we can get a clearer picture of our own predicament here on earth if we look at what is going on, or imagined to be going on, in outer space, or what the Bible prefers to call 'heaven'.

For god to be in heaven means that although he is beyond our control, he is not totally beyond our comprehension. We may see only one side of the moon, but that is enough to know that the other side is there even if we are not entirely sure what it is like. So it is with God. We know enough about him to be assured that he exists, but there are large areas we cannot see and that will always remain beyond our grasp in this life. Is it possible to know about God without receiving a special revelation from him? The Bible says it is – the heavens declare the glory of God, says the psalmist, and the sky above shows his handiwork (Ps. 19:1). Only the fool says that there is no God; an awareness of his existence is rooted in every human being (Ps. 14:1; Rom. 1:20–21). Certainly, it is true that every known human culture has some awareness of a higher power governing the universe, and although modern atheists have tried to stamp it out, belief in such a power continues to flourish in any number of different forms. God has not left himself without a witness, and as long as the heavens are visible we may be certain that some form of belief in him will survive.

Of course, belief of that kind is not enough for convinced Christians. It is possible for anyone to be aware of the existence of a higher power, but that is not the same thing as knowing God in the biblical sense. We may perhaps compare this natural know-ledge to seeing a black man standing at the bus stop. As a passer-by I will be aware of certain things about him – that he is male, for example, and that he probably comes from a part of the world in which black people are numerous. That much I might rea-sonably guess, but I would have little way of knowing any more about him, and even what I think I know might turn out to be wrong. The only way to find out for sure is to ask the man himself who he is and where he comes from – and to be prepared for a surprise if it turns out that random guessing on the basis of probabilities is incorrect. Similarly, we may be able to surmise that such a being as God exists and we may guess that he is our Creator, but beyond that we can know nothing certain about him unless he chooses to reveal himself to us.

Even then, we must accept that our capacity for understanding this revelation will not be great enough to encompass the whole reality. When we meet other people and they reveal themselves to us, we learn something about them, but there is always much more that remains hidden from our eyes. It is even true to say that we do not understand ourselves very deeply, so how can we expect to plumb the depths of God? The history of theology is full of failed attempts to reconcile things we know about him that remain beyond our comprehension. We do not know precisely how his love and justice go together, though we can be sure they do. We cannot understand how divine predestination can allow for human free will, but we know it does. It puzzles us how God can be everywhere and yet come into our hearts as if he were not there before, but that is how we experience him. These things are paradoxes to us, but they are reminders that God goes beyond the limits of our finite minds, which struggle to absorb the concept of the infinite, let alone its presence in our lives.

It is most important to insist that when we say that the heavens are high above the earth, and confess that we who are bound to the latter cannot hope to penetrate more than the surface of them, we are not limiting ourselves to the physical universe. It is said that Yuri Gagarin, the first man to travel in space, came back claiming that he had not seen any sign of God there. The story may well not be true, but if it is, it displays a remarkably limited understanding of reality. Christians understand perfectly well that we can travel down the Milky Way and back without ever encountering God in a physical sense, for the simple reason that God is not physical. At the same time, we also know that there is no need to go that far, or indeed to go anywhere at all, because God's existence is of a completely different kind. Professional atheists like to claim that they have conducted endless scientific experiments, none of which has revealed God, and are surprised when Christians react to the news with complete equanimity. From our point of view, the really worrying thing would be if they claimed to have encountered him in that way, because whatever they had come across could not possibly be God as we understand him!

As a spiritual being, God can only be met in a spiritual way. All human beings have a spiritual side to them, as the universal existence of both religion and superstition attests. It is not widely known, but one of the more curious things about the Soviet Union, especially in its latter years, was the way in which the state authorities encouraged superstitious beliefs as a means of heading off what they saw as a more dangerous interest in religious truth. The thought of Communist Party members studying their horoscopes seems bizarre to us, but so it was – and so it still is in our supposedly 'secular' Western societies as well, where even respectable newspapers carry such details. The widespread popularity of consciousness-altering drugs, magic and fairy tales about Narnia, Middle Earth or even Hogwarts, bears witness to the human thirst for the spiritual, whether this has any connection to objective reality or not. Recently, a primary-school teacher in England was officially reprimanded for telling his nine-year-old pupils that there is no Santa Claus. This might seem to be unnecessarily churlish behaviour on the teacher's part, but it is hard to disagree with him at the strictly factual level. The really surprising thing about this incident was that many of the parents who protested against him did so because they wanted their children's belief in Santa to be protected, and the reason many of them gave for that was that they believed in him themselves!

Christians have long understood that they are engaged in a spiritual warfare with such superstitions, and that it is impossible simply to legislate them out of existence. The early church is sometimes criticized for its propensity to 'baptize' paganism by turning sacred sites into places of Christian pilgrimage, but whatever we think about some of the things they did, we should not forget that the main purpose of this was to claim the territory occupied by false gods and redeem it for the truth. This was why the Parthenon, originally dedicated to the virgin goddess Athena,

---

9. *Parthenos* is the Greek word for 'virgin'.

became the church of St Mary the Virgin.[9] It is why the winter festival of the dying and rising light was transformed into Christmas, the feast of the coming of the true Light into the world. Today we live in a time when the Christian overlay given to such festivals is regarded by many as politically incorrect and offensive to unbelievers, but what happens when the Christian content is removed? The answer is that these festivals do not go away; on the contrary, their pagan underlay tends to resurface with a vengeance. This is particularly obvious (and painful) at Easter, an event clearly recorded in the Bible as the resurrection of Christ, but which is celebrated today mainly with eggs and bunnies – a reminder that the Christian feast replaced an earlier fertility cult to which the name 'Easter' continues to bear witness.[10] Obviously, the church occasionally went too far in trying to baptize pagan rituals, as when it famously invented 'St Denis', who is none other than the pagan god Dionysus dressed up to look like a Christian martyr, but such excesses should not blind us to the very real problem we have to face. If we abandon all earthly manifestations of spirituality on the ground that such manifestations are finite and therefore idolatrous, there is every likelihood that they will be taken over by superstitious forces, and that the latter state will prove to be worse than the first.

Christian spirituality is not superstition but reality. The beliefs and practices of other religions and pseudo-religions bear witness to the spiritual dimension of human life but their content is a caricature of this truth. Furthermore, Christian spirituality is not disincarnate – far from it! The whole message of Jesus Christ is that 'the Word became flesh and dwelt among us, and we have seen his glory' – in the flesh (John 1:14)! God accommodates himself to our finite minds, showing us what we need to know about him in ways we are capable of taking in.

---

10. ' Easter' was the pagan Anglo-Saxon goddess of the east, the rising sun and fertility. The name has spread to the Germanic countries of northern Europe, which were largely evangelized from England; most of the others prefer to use a variant of *pascha*, the Greek version of Hebrew *pesach*, or 'Passover'.

That there is so much more to know we should not doubt, but that fact alone does not discredit the information we have, any more than our limited knowledge of the universe discredits the rest. What we know is accurate within the parameters we have to work with, and God accepts we can act only within the bounds he has set for us. The rest will become clear in due course, when we go to join him in heaven and become capable of seeing him as he really is. To believe that God is in heaven is to accept that he knows us in a way we do not know ourselves. Recently, I flew over my birthplace and saw a quarry not far from my home which I had always known was there, but which I had never actually seen. I had no idea how deep it was, or what the rock formations revealed by the digging looked like, and could not relate it to other things in the area. Suddenly, as I looked down from the air, the whole thing was laid out before my eyes and I saw my own familiar neighbourhood in a way I had never seen it before. Magnify this by a factor of many millions and you may get some idea of how God looks at us. Things in and around us, of which we may be aware at some level of our being but of which we have no real knowledge, to him are both perfectly clear and in proper perspective.

As long as we remain in this life, we shall never be able to see things from God's vantage point. To help us overcome this disadvantage, he has to communicate his mind to us in a way we can understand. When God uses the physical heavens to speak to us about the spiritual heaven in which he dwells, he does so by a process we call 'analogy'. Some people believe it is possible to take certain qualities of the physical heaven – its vast size for example – and extrapolate from them to our understanding of God. Mathematicians often talk about 'infinity', a word Christians immediately recognize, but we have to remember that the difference between the mathematical use of this term and the theological one is not one of degree – it is one of kind. God is not more infinite than mathematical infinity; he is infinite in a different way. Mathematical infinity can help us to understand and express this, but only because we recognize that it has certain affinities to what we really want to say. When we reach the point where we can no longer use mathematical infinity to understand God's nature, we say that the analogy has broken down, and some other form of explanation has to be devised. Christians understand this because we have received a revelation from God that makes sense in its own terms, even if we are forced to describe it in other ways. We know when the limits have been reached because our experience of spiritual reality tells us what they are.

There is a remarkable consensus among Christians on this point, which is powerful evidence, even if it is not absolute scientific 'proof', that the claims made for the existence of God are true. It is a dimension of reality closed to scientific observation, but it is no less real for that. The 'proof' we have to offer is the evidence of the changed lives of those who have come to know God in Christ and who have been radically transformed by him. It is a change immediately recognizable to those who have experienced it, and it transcends cultural, temporal and even theological barriers. Christians differ about many things, but those who have met the living God have a bond that unites them in spite of everything. The key to understanding this is submission. If we insist on making God conform to notions we can make sense of and are prepared to accept, we shall never know him. Philosophers of every age have tried to do this but have all failed, even when the theories they have put forward sound plausible enough at first sight. The so-called 'proofs for the existence of God' can provide some intellectual comfort to those who already believe, but they cannot lead a person to faith. Only the Holy Spirit of God can do that, and when he does, all pretence of human wisdom pales before him. The Holy Spirit speaks in spiritual terms to those who are spiritual, giving them an understanding of divine things, which opens the gates of heaven to them, even before taking us there to dwell with him for ever.

Spiritual knowledge of this kind is the essential precondition for receiving spiritual power. God is not only able to intervene in our lives as and when he chooses, but he can do this in the right way because he sees the whole picture at once – something not available to us. By praying to God in heaven we are recognizing his knowledge and power, which he exercises with wisdom and benevolence towards us precisely because he is our Father. By praying to God in heaven, we are also recognizing that he is sovereign over everything on earth. The word 'sovereignty' literally means 'aboveness', *superanitas* in the original Latin, and it is this aboveness that is the determining factor in his authority over us. We are subject to him, but he is subject to no-one, and so to know him is to know the one who ultimately governs and controls our lives.

What is more, the Father who dwells in heaven cannot be brought down to earth. He cannot be knocked off his throne, he can never lose his sovereignty. He sends his Son into the world, and his Holy Spirit comes into our hearts, but the Father remains out of reach as a reminder to us of what God in his essence is and must be like. In himself, he is completely different from us, dwelling in another world according to different principles of existence. Where he is, there is no time and no space, neither is there death nor any form of evil or suffering. It is quite literally another universe, one that we can imagine to the extent it is described to us, but that our human finitude makes impossible for us to experience directly.

Some people find this unacceptable, and do not want a God who is above and beyond our human concerns. To their minds, God becomes real only when he comes down to our level, and if he cannot do that, then he must be abandoned in favour of some other being who can. At the present time, this view is expressed most loudly by those who say God can and must be able to suffer, because if suffering is alien to his being, he must be alien to us. The logic of this sounds persuasive at first sight, and many have fallen for its seductiveness, but a little reflection will show it is untenable. It is certainly true that the human predicament demands a God who understands what is wrong with us, and no Christian has ever denied that. But it also requires a God who can stand back from the situation far enough to be able to do something about it. A doctor helps his patients by showing sympathy for their sufferings, but this does not mean he has to undergo them himself. Indeed, we would probably lose confidence in any physician who felt he had to share our disease before being able to cure us. We are not interested in this; what we want is to be released from our troubles, and the chances are that someone who is *not* suffering as we are will be better placed to do this. Think of someone who has fallen down a well or been trapped in a mine-shaft and ask yourself where the most effective rescuer is likely to come from. Not, surely, from someone foolish enough to throw himself down into the pit to show his solidarity with the victim! Loose thinking like this is widespread today, but when we hear this kind of talk, we must remember that our Father is in heaven, above and beyond our current troubles and therefore better placed than anyone else to do something about them. If God were no more than the supreme being, he might well be indifferent and impervious to our plight, but he is our Father and, because of that, he comes to our rescue. His sovereignty as the supreme being then appears as a vitally important aid to facilitate his rescue operation, not as a barrier preventing him from ever getting involved with us.

Hallowed be your name

The power and sovereignty of God are revealed most fully and most clearly in his name. This seems strange to the modern mind, particularly in Western countries, where names have lost any particular significance. How many of us can say, for example, what our own name means? Some people bear names that have come down through the family, while others may simply follow fashion with little thought for anything else. In traditionally Christian societies, babies may still be named for the saint on whose day they were born or baptized. That was certainly the case with Martin Luther, who was baptized on St Martin's Day (11 November) in 1483 and so was almost certainly born sometime in the preceding twenty-four hours. Surnames are often more easily understandable, and presumably they reflect some past reality, but how many people called Taylor or Smith exercise those professions now? And who would suppose that someone called Johnson was the son of John, or Thompson, the son of Thomas?[11] These names became fossilized many centuries ago and it would not occur to us to attach any real meaning to them now.

---

11. This tradition is still preserved in Iceland, however, where family names as we know them are rare.

In biblical times things were very different. It is well known that
the ancient Israelites paid far more attention to names than we do
today. At significant moments in the history of God's people we
discover that names intended to be prophetic witnesses of that
nation's destiny were given. 'You will conceive in your womb and
bear a son, and you shall call his name Jesus' (Luke 1:31). You do
not have to go very far in Scripture before you will discover that
the names given to people generally have a direct association
with their identity. 'Adam' was someone formed from the earth
(*adamah*). 'Eve' was so called because she was the mother of all
living things (*havah*). Abram (father of a nation) had his name
changed to Abraham (father of a great nation) as a prophetic sign
that God's covenant with him would be fulfilled in that way (Gen.
17:5). Jacob, his grandson, became Israel, because he wrestled with
God and prevailed (Gen. 32:28). Names not only reflected the
character of those who bore them, but presented them with a
challenge to live up to. This is clear in the New Testament, where
Jesus called Simon from his fishing boat and named him Cephas
(Peter), because despite all his manifest failings, he would become
the rock on which the church would be built (John 1:42; Matt.
16:18–19).

When Jesus told his disciples to pray for the hallowing of God's
name, he knew they would understand this had ramifications that
went far beyond mere nomenclature. God's name was not just a
label, but a sign that spoke of his character, of his authority and of
his purposes for the world he had made and the people he had
called and chosen to be his. It is for this reason Jesus tells us to
keep it holy, both in theory and in practice. What does this mean?
Is God not holy already? Why are we being asked to pray for
something that seems to be an intrinsic part of his nature? Here
we have to stop and think about what it means to be 'holy'.
Holiness is not a quality inherent in a thing, like weight or visibility.
To be 'holy' is to be set apart, kept distinct, recognized as of
special value and worth. It is often said that God is holy in himself,
but strictly speaking this is not so, because without someone or
something else to compare him with, the word has no meaning. It
is possible for God to be called holy only in relation to other
things, and this is why we are told to hallow his name. In ordinary

human experience, God is one factor to be considered among many others, and because he is invisible, he is seldom the one that strikes us most obviously. Many people go through life without giving God a second thought, even if they theoretically believe in him, because he does not seem real in their everyday lives. At best, he is a last resort, to be appealed to when all else fails. It is hardly surprising that such prayers of desperation are seldom answered, but no-one can deny that they are common, and reflect what many people think about God.

This is why it is so important for us to make a special effort to keep God's name holy. If we fail to do this, we shall lose sight of him altogether. One of the surest and saddest forms of unbelief is the way in which so many people let God's name slip off their tongues in utterances that are blasphemous because, as the third commandment puts it, they are literally 'taking God's name in vain' (Exod. 20:7). Perhaps without realizing what they are doing, they are appealing to the power who lies behind the universe and dragging him down to the level of their own frustrated anger. Can we be surprised if God says he will hold this against those who do such a thing? You cannot play with fire without getting burned, and, as the Bible says, our God is a consuming fire (Heb. 12:29). Blaspheming God's name in no way diminishes him but it compromises those who resort to such practices and blinds them to the truth they will one day have to face at the judgment.

God's name is holy from our perspective, because it is meant to be set apart in our minds and specially honoured by us. It is of particular importance because it identifies both who he is and what he is. In the early church, people who thought deeply about God were primarily concerned to define what he was – invisible, immortal, impassible and so on. His attributes are manifold and absolute, unique in their splendour and perfection. Understood in this way, God is totally different from us, indeed the very opposite of what we are. As we have already suggested, his otherness is essential to his being and must at all costs be preserved if we are to do justice to him. If we try to bring him down to our level, we end up creating something that is no more than a caricature of the real thing. A god we can handle is no god at all but an idol of our imagination. It may give us some kind of comfort, rather like a rabbit's foot or some other talisman of good luck, but it will let us down badly when we need its help because it is entirely lacking in power. The true God shatters all our images of him because these images are barriers and constraints to our relationship with him. Only when I accept that he can do anything, whether I think it is possible or not, will I begin to appreciate the presence of his power in my life. Only then, indeed, will I really start to understand what it means to regard his name as holy.

What God is inevitably distances him from us, but paradoxically, *who* he is draws us closer to him. Perhaps for this reason, the Bible says relatively little about what God is, but concentrates instead on him as a personal being, a 'who' who relates directly to us. As our Father, he has created us in his image and given us the power to communicate with him, if not as equals, then at least on the same wavelength. For we too are persons, the only creatures to whom that designation is specifically given. Angels are individuals with personal characteristics, but they are not created in the image and likeness of God, and on the last day we shall sit in judgment over them. We have been called to an altogether special destiny, to a place at his side in heaven that is far above anything granted to another creature, however spiritual and exalted that creature might be. By hallowing his name we protect that relationship and remind ourselves of its centrality in our lives and future destiny.

But what exactly is God's name? It is certainly not the word 'god', a term that can be applied to any being claiming divine status (and there were many of those in Jesus' day). Unlike Islam, which insists on using the name 'Allah' for God in every language, Christianity has been content to take whatever name is suitable for the purpose of describing the supreme being in the language of the people whom it is evangelizing, and that is what has happened in English. 'Lord' is another title given to God, but it too is not exclusive to him, and can be used in many different contexts. Very often it is the term of choice for translating the Hebrew *YHWH* (Yahweh), the name by which God made himself known to Moses at the burning bush and that is generally translated 'He who is' (Exod. 3:14). In that sense it possesses a uniqueness hidden from view by the general habit, which goes back to ancient times and was respected by the New Testament writers, of not pronouncing the name of God itself. In that case, of course, the word 'Lord' is not God's name, but a substitute for it – ultimately a form of concealment rather than of revelation.

The God whom we worship is the absolute Being, before whom there is none greater. For this reason, his uniqueness is conveyed to us, not in the words 'god' or 'lord', but in the great title Almighty, which translates the Hebrew *El-Shaddai* and the Greek *Pantokratōr*. In the ancient world there were many gods and many lords, but there could only ever be one Almighty. In that single word are summed up his sovereignty, power and uniqueness – all the characteristics we must keep before our eyes as we seek to hallow his name.

The name of God thus identifies him to us as the one who has made us, who preserves us and who will save us for eternity. To exalt this name is to proclaim his power and make known his love, because it is as the Almighty that he is our Father – we believe in God, the Father, the Almighty, maker of heaven and earth, as the Nicene Creed puts it. The name of God inspires fear – not the terror of fright but the respect that issues in reverence. When we hear it, we are reminded of his majesty and glory, of the great works he has done for us in the past and of the promises he has stored up for us in the future.

We hallow God's name because of who he is, and in hallowing it, we are hallowing ourselves as well. God's name is set apart from ordinary human intercourse, and as we draw closer to him and treasure his name more and more, we are lifted out of our everyday concerns and united to his eternal glory. The significance of this is brought out in the New Testament by the apostle Paul, who remarks that the Jewish people bear the name of God, which is blasphemed throughout the world because of their unworthy behaviour (Rom. 2:24). Christians bear the name of Christ, and if we do not live up to our high calling, then we also are guilty of failing to hallow his name. It is one of the saddest witnesses of our failure to do this that in so many places the name 'Christian' is regarded with slight amusement, if not with open contempt. Who do these people think they are? They preach a religion of love and peace, yet are constantly at each other's throats. They profess one of the loftiest moral codes ever to have been devised, yet many of their leaders are mired in scandal. Hardly a day goes by but a popular newspaper is carrying another story of how a Christian or a church has fallen into some form of sin. In extreme cases, like Northern Ireland or the countries of the former Yugoslavia, sectarian violence has claimed the lives of thousands and the official churches seem to be unable to intervene effectively to rebuke their so-called flocks. All over the world we find one Christian group at odds with another, often within the same church structures. Paul's remarks about the Jews of his day have an uncomfortable ring to them when we look around and see how the professed servants of Christ can sometimes behave.

Perhaps never more than in the current media age, we have a duty to remember what the wider social implications of hallowing the name of God are. One area of vital concern here is the need for church discipline, which in most cases has all but broken down. Afraid as we are of losing members, and reluctant as we are to pass judgment on fellow sinners, we have gradually become tolerant of almost anything and everything. It is true that Jesus came to call sinners and not the righteous, but he came to call them to repentance, not to affirm them in their misbehaviour and encourage them to carry on as before. Our churches will always be full of moral and spiritual failures, people who return again and again for the forgiveness we so desperately need. But having said that, the New Testament is quite clear that the Christian church must maintain certain standards in its public life so as not to bring the gospel of Christ into disrepute. The apostle Paul was quite insistent that the church's worship should be conducted decently and in order for this very reason. He did not object to people who spoke in tongues or exercised other unusual spiritual gifts, but he insisted that they should be kept under control, and on no account were they to monopolize the gatherings of God's people. Given a choice, the apostle preferred to speak five words in a language people could understand and benefit from than ten thousand in an unknown tongue (1 Cor. 14:40). Public worship is by definition evangelistic because it is a statement to the outside world of what we believe. If we approach it without due reverence, then we can be sure that the message which will be conveyed is that we have nothing worth offering to anyone else. Sadly, too many people

today are so preoccupied with expressing themselves in worship
that they have completely forgotten the impression it leaves on
others who may not find it so easy to enter into the spirit of the
occasion. Without going to the point of suppressing spontaneity
entirely, we desperately need to recover a sense of the holiness of
God in our public proclamation of him, remembering that what
we say will be confirmed or denied by the way in which we put it
across.

Moral failings are another obvious source of trouble and the
unwillingness to deal adequately with sexual misdemeanours is as
common today as it was in ancient Corinth. Statistics have shown
that there is no noticeable difference in the divorce rate among
churchgoers as compared with the general population, which is a
matter of great shame to us. The trouble is that each divorce makes
the next one easier to accept, and we have now reached a situation
where clear teaching on the subject is very difficult because so
many members of our congregations have been divorced and are
therefore liable to take exception to it. Homosexual unions are not
only tolerated, but they are sometimes encouraged, even among
the clergy. In the Church of England at least, and no doubt
elsewhere as well, it is possible for a clergyman to undergo a sex-
change operation and remain in post, no questions asked. Anyone
who dares to object to this state of affairs is immediately shouted
down as 'homophobic', 'unloving' or worse. It is not for us to pass
judgment on such people – judgment belongs to God. But we
have a duty to maintain certain standards in the accredited ministers of the church, however far short of them we often fall. There
is all the difference in the world between a sinner who repents and
seeks forgiveness and restoration, and an activist who sees nothing
wrong with his behaviour and who is striking a blow for moral
degradation in the name of 'freedom'. Tragically, so many of our
churches are being hollowed out from within because we are afraid
to exercise the proper discipline needed to hallow the name of
God in the way it is meant to be.

'Hallowed be your name' is therefore not a prayer for change or
improvement in God, but for change and improvement in us. In
praying for his name to be set apart for special honour we are
really praying for ourselves, asking that we may be made worthy

bearers of it, genuine witnesses to the love that sacrificed itself so
that we might be cleansed from our sins and enabled to stand
in the heavenly places with him. Beyond the public manifestations
of this, which are so vitally necessary for the health and welfare of
the church, there is the equally important calling each of us has to
make this truth a reality in our own lives. None of us is perfect,
and as long as we live in this world there will be room for improvement. God does not expect us to be better than we are capable of
being, and he is always on hand to forgive and restore us when we
fail. What he wants from us is the right approach and the right
attitude. The wisdom of the world tells us that our days are numbered, but only in the Bible do we find the prayer 'So teach us to
number our days that we may get a heart of wisdom' (Ps. 90:12).
What other peoples regard as an inescapable fate, Jews and
Christians see as a learning opportunity. The time is limited, so let
us make the most of it. There is all the difference in the world
between people who wander about aimlessly from one thing to
another and those who calculate the time available to them and
establish their priorities accordingly. God has chosen us to be his
witnesses in the world, where our behaviour will either sanctify or
blaspheme his name. May he grant us the grace to hallow that
name in our lives and so fulfil the prayer Jesus taught us to pray.

2. YOUR KINGDOM COME, YOUR WILL BE DONE ON EARTH AS IT IS IN HEAVEN

The king and the kingdom

New Testament scholars differ about many things, but even the most radical sceptics among them agree that there were two key elements in the teaching of Jesus. The first of these is that he taught the fatherhood of God, which we looked at in the last chapter, and the second is that he preached the coming of the kingdom, though there is considerable disagreement about what he meant by that. Until the twentieth century, language of that kind would have been easily understood, since most countries in the world were still monarchies of one kind or another. Today they have largely disappeared, and the ones that remain are usually constitutional democracies in which the role of the monarch is mainly ceremonial and symbolic. This does not mean that the phenomenon of one-person rule has ceased to exist, of course, but nowadays it is much cruder and often considerably more vicious than most traditional monarchies were. In the twentieth century, ancient states like Russia, China, Iran and Ethiopia lost their monarchs only to find themselves saddled with something far worse, from which they are only beginning to emerge. In many parts of the developing world, dictatorships succeed one another with monotonous regularity, and often seem to outsiders to be competing to see which of them can be the most tyrannical. Elsewhere, the lure of kingship remains powerful, even in Western democracies – for example, not even the most determined republican ideologue would say that Elvis Presley was the president of rock and roll!

Kingship, where it still exists, almost always has a religious dimension. This is true in European countries, where the monarchs usually have a special relationship with the state church, which survives as such as least partly because the monarch belongs to it. Few people now remember it, but in both Britain and France it was for many centuries the custom for the king to touch people suffering from scrofula, the disease popularly known as 'the king's evil', because it was believed that the royal touch would bring about a cure. The practice was discontinued in Britain after the death of Queen Anne in 1714, but it is interesting to note that it was maintained by the Stuart pretenders throughout the eighteenth century, as the ultimate proof that they, and not the Hanoverian Georges, were the legitimate kings.[1] This semi-magical religious dimension is certainly present in the case of Elvis, whose cult resembles that of a medieval saint. It is hardly an accident that it is focused around his mansion near Memphis, which is revealingly called Graceland – a religious term if ever there was one!

When we turn to the ancient world, the links between kings and religious worship are so universal that it is the exceptions that are remarkable. The Roman Empire was one of these, at least up to a point. The Romans did not accept that their emperors were gods, so they compromised with the beliefs of their subject peoples and allowed themselves to claim that dead emperors were deified. Their living successors however had to be content to be known as sons of a god, not as gods themselves. This distinction was a fine

---

1. In France, the custom died out in the mid-eighteenth century, only to be revived for the coronation of Charles X in 1825. After the French Revolution, Charles needed to advertise his legitimacy, and what better way to do it than this?

one though, especially in the eastern parts of the empire where the cult of the ruler was long established. When Jesus told Pilate that his kingdom was not of this world, his words may have increased fears of a political uprising rather than quelled them, since the Romans had only recently conquered territories where the worship of divine kings had gone on for centuries. Pilate seems to have been unimpressed with Jesus' claims to kingship and regarded him as innocent, but even so, such claims were bound to appear seditious to some people. We must not forget that when Jesus was crucified, Pilate wrote on the cross that he was 'king of the Jews', as if that claim in itself were enough to merit his gruesome fate. The Jews objected, even going to the point of hypocritically protesting their loyalty to Caesar, but Pilate would not be deflected from advertising what to him must have been the only real ground for Jesus' condemnation. Whether (or in what sense) it was true did not concern him, but if the fate meted out to Jesus served to discourage anyone else from trying something similar, then so much the better (John 19:12–22).

In the Old Testament, kingship appears in a somewhat ambiguous light. The Israelites were slow to establish a monarchy, and when they finally did so it was made clear to them that they were rebelling against God, who was their true king (1 Sam. 8:4–18). The initial experiment with Saul was a disaster, but it is interesting to note that God did not persuade the people to return to the age of the judges. Instead, he chose another king for them, the shepherd David, and promised him that his descendants would rule the house of Israel for ever. If Jesus was entitled to call himself the king of the Jews it was because he was the son of David, born in Bethlehem and a direct descendant, legally through Joseph and physically through Mary, of Israel's greatest king.[2] From the very beginning, his royal descent and potential claims to the throne of Israel are a major theme of the Gospels, far outweighing any references to his high-priestly role as the final and perfect sacrifice. That is developed more fully in the epistle to the Hebrews, but

---

2. This point is brought out very clearly in the genealogy given in Matt. 1:1–17.

there can be little doubt that the biographical material in the New Testament relating to Jesus shows a strong tendency to concentrate on his role as the coming king as the chief way in which he would fulfil the promises made in the Old Testament.

Kingship may have been disapproved of when it was first introduced into Israel, but it did not take long for it to develop a religious dimension of its own. Psalm 45 provides an excellent example of this:

My heart overflows with a pleasing theme;
    I address my verses to the king;
    my tongue is like the pen of a ready scribe.

You are the most handsome of the sons of men;
    grace is poured upon your lips;
    therefore God has blessed you forever.
Gird your sword on your thigh, O mighty one,
    in your splendour and majesty!
. . .
Your throne, O God, is forever and ever.
    The sceptre of your kingdom is a sceptre of uprightness;
you have loved righteousness and hated wickedness.
Therefore God, your God, has anointed you
    with the oil of gladness beyond your companions.
(Psalm 45:1–3, 6–7)

The immediate subject of the psalm is the king of Israel, but the language used of him shows how close he is to God, and in verse 6 it appears that he is actually addressed as God! How was this possible? Unlike the nations round about, Israel never acknowledged the divinity of its kings and remained firmly committed to the worship of the one true God. Psalm 45 stands in that tradition, so much so that Christians have usually interpreted these verses as referring primarily to Christ the king, the one who is at the same time both God and man. Furthermore, the prophets of ancient Israel did not hesitate to condemn their kings when they did things of which God did not approve, and the common epitaph that the books of the kings records, 'He did what was evil in the sight of the LORD',[3] is one of the most chilling obituary notices ever penned. But even so, and in spite of the many failings of its leading representatives, the degree to which the Davidic monarchy was assimilated to the kingdom of God is striking and reminds us that the claims of Jesus have deep roots in the worshipping life of ancient Israel.

Your kingdom come

Jesus tells us to pray to the Father for the coming of his kingdom. How can this be, when the Father is the Sovereign Lord of the universe, the one who upholds everything by the power of his word and without whose permission nothing can come to pass? How can his kingdom come when it is already present everywhere we look? To understand this we need to consider the spiritual context Jesus was addressing, in which we still live. Hard as it is to understand, the Sovereign Lord of all has created beings capable of rebelling against him, and, at some unknown point, that is precisely what happened. The Bible does not fully explain this, but from inferences here and there we glean that long before the creation of the world, the highest of the angelic creatures wanted to usurp the place of God, and in so doing this created being fell from his exalted position (cf. Ezek. 28:12–19). This was Satan, or the devil as he is commonly known, who was not destroyed for his rebellion but confined to a restricted sphere of operation that Scripture usually refers to as 'the world'.[4]

Soon after the creation of man in the Garden of Eden, Satan appeared in the form of a serpent and tempted Adam and Eve to join him in his rebellion. Our first parents were promised that if they heeded the serpent, they would become like God, as indeed they did to some degree (Gen. 3:5). Their disobedience gave them a knowledge of good and evil they had not previously had, and in order to prevent them living forever, God expelled them from the

---

3. See 1 Kgs 22:52 and many similar instances.

4. Like 'heaven', but in diametrical opposition to it, this word is used in Scripture with two meanings, a physical and a moral/spiritual one.

garden and barred them from the tree of life. To their dismay, Adam and Eve found that they had been consigned to the kingdom of Satan, the prince of this world. Because of that, all of their descendants, including you and me, now belong to it as well.

What is the kingdom of Satan like? Fundamentally, it is illegitimate, a rogue state holding a restricted spiritual territory at the pleasure of the true ruler, God. Satan and his demonic hosts are perfectly conscious of this, but their ability to deceive is such that their human hostages are unaware of it. Perhaps there are some human beings who have found out the truth and have decided to sell their souls to Satan completely, as the legend of Faust suggests, but if so, the Bible says nothing about it. The impression we get from Scripture is that fallen human beings have no relationship with Satan comparable to the relationship Adam and Eve had with God in the Garden of Eden. The Genesis story may suggest otherwise, but this is probably yet another deception on Satan's part. He spoke to the first human beings in a way that suggested he was their friend, but once they were in his power, he abandoned them and they had no further contact of that kind. For the most part, human beings nowadays are unaware of their captivity because they have never experienced anything else. They know they will die, of course, and sense this is a tragedy, so may try to escape from their destiny by seeking some form of eternal life. In this respect, Satan gives them an illusion of freedom, which makes it possible for them to work out elaborate schemes of salvation that promise deliverance to those who follow them to the letter, if they can. The problem of course is that they cannot – the challenge they face is simply too great for any humanly devised scheme to be able to overcome it. Satan knows this but encourages the delusion because it has the effect of blinding his captives to the truth.

The truth, however, is that there is no escape from within his kingdom. The kingdom of Satan can be defeated only from outside, by the operation of God himself. In what we call the Old Testament, God reached out to some of Satan's captives and made them his agents behind enemy lines. These were the people of Israel, who were chosen to be a light to the nations and a witness to the power of the true God. Israel was never highly regarded by the other peoples of antiquity, and for much of the time it did not deserve to be, since it was more likely to fall into the ways of Satan's world than to resist them as it could and should have done. In some ways, Israel may be compared to the French Resistance in the Second World War – conscious of its mission, occasionally effective, but constantly subject to betrayal from within its ranks and ultimately incapable of winning without outside help. This help finally came in Jesus Christ, the Son of God sent into the world by his Father in order to do battle with the kingdom of Satan, overcome it and set the captives free.

This is where we come in. When Jesus taught his disciples how to pray he had already met the enemy and repelled him, but the battle was not yet fully joined. The disciples did not realize it at the time, but they were being called to join his fight against the devil. After his victory it would be their task to proclaim his triumph throughout the world and rally men and women to his standard. We who look back on these events from the vantage point of two thousand years of hindsight can see all this, but it must have seemed very different to people at that time. For a start, most of Israel failed to understand what was happening and rejected him completely. The Jews had been told about his coming but it was a coded message they failed to interpret correctly. The promised Messiah was in their midst but they were unable to recognize him because they had got the signals wrong. They were expecting a new David, someone who would come from nowhere, rally the troops and slay the giants of Rome. As oppressed people often do, they blamed everything that was wrong with them on their oppressors, and imagined that getting rid of them would be enough to usher in the golden age. Today we have seen enough of this kind of thing to know it is a delusion, and if anyone had succeeded in doing what Jewish popular sentiment wanted, the experiment would have ended in tears and the whole messianic idea would have been discredited. But this is the wisdom of experience, and the Jews of Jesus' day still felt free to fantasize about something that effectively remained outside the bounds of practical politics. Rebellion against the Romans did indeed come a generation after Jesus' ministry, but it was a disaster from the start and led only to the destruction of the

Jerusalem temple and whatever vestiges of Jewish national identity had managed to survive until then.

In telling the story of Jewish messianism in the time of Jesus,
the New Testament writers bring out another factor that the
Jews themselves would never have been able to admit. Despite
their protests to the contrary, the truth was that they had grown
used to their spiritual situation and did not really want to be
delivered from it. For reasons both good and bad, they preferred
to remain an elite resistance movement on hostile territory rather
than join any victorious army of liberation. Their struggle gave
them their identity, bonded them together and produced great
feats of endurance, all of which would disappear if they were
simply to be merged into the allied forces of the Lord. This
attitude was not hard to justify; after all, how could they be sure
that Jesus was the answer they had been waiting for without
seeing the results? It was better for them to stay as they were, and
to go on following battle instructions that they knew had
come from God, rather than risk obeying a new message that in
the end might turn out to be no more than a clever deception of
the enemy.

The disciples of Jesus had been brought up in these resistance
circles, and their willingness to break with them is extraordinary,
especially as it must have been difficult for them to see what Jesus
was getting at. Somehow they had come to believe that he was the
deliverer whom God had promised, but as the Gospels tell us,
they had little idea of what that meant in practice. Most of the
time it appears that they thought that Jesus was the standard
Jewish Messiah figure who had come to establish a political
kingdom that would crush the other nations under its feet. It
never seems to have occurred to them that if that had happened,
the kingdom of Jesus would not have been the kingdom of God
but simply a more effective agent of the kingdom of Satan – just
as worldly empires and powers have always been. The messianic
empire might have been a pleasant place to live in, especially for
Jews who would presumably have become the ruling class, but the
whole thing would have been a fraud and in the end it would have
come crashing down as other empires before and ever since have
done.

One of the problems was that Jesus had a strategy for winning that was incomprehensible, even to his closest followers. Instead of attacking Satan head-on, he undertook occasional raids into his territory, healing the sick and curing the demon-possessed, but made little further advance in the course of his earthly ministry. Satan was able to stir up powerful resistance against him and so ensured that instead of joining forces with Jesus, the Jewish leaders of the day would do the devil's work instead. He even managed to plant an agent among Jesus' disciples – Judas Iscariot, whose status as their treasurer showed that he was among the most trusted of the group (John 13:29). Jesus knew all this, but, far from trying to escape Satan's clutches, allowed himself to be drawn into what must have looked very much like a trap. When the moment was ripe, Judas betrayed him, the leaders of Israel condemned him and the Roman authorities, fearing the consequences if they stood back and watched, obligingly put him to death. Little did they know that by doing this they were actually fulfilling Jesus' own strategy for victory over the enemy.

Satan did not realize until it was too late that the Son of God had come into the world not to take him on in open combat but to subvert his kingdom from within. Jesus did this by appropriating to himself everything Satan had managed to achieve – the combined sins of the human race, in other words. In a figurative but still effective sense, Jesus became sin for us and confronted the devil on his own territory by dying and putting that sin to death along with himself (2 Cor. 5:21). On the cross of Calvary, the work Satan had built up over millennia was overthrown in a single afternoon. The battle lasted six hours, but when it was over, Satan's kingdom lay in ruins because its greatest, and indeed its only real, achievement had been wiped out. All that remained was a mop-up operation that began, appropriately enough, in hell, the spiritual place Satan claimed as his preserve and where he held dead human beings captive. By going there to preach his message of deliverance, Jesus showed there was no stronghold he could not penetrate, no barrier he could not overcome, no soul he could not reach. Those who belonged to him heard his voice and responded to his call, while those who did not were confirmed in their rebellion and rendered powerless to do anything to harm those who were being saved.[5]

On the third day Jesus came back from the dead, and forty days later went up to heaven with his booty in tow (Eph. 4:8). He then sat down at the right hand of the Father and began his glorious reign in heaven. This reign will continue until the end of time when everything will finally be wrapped up and he will present his kingdom, fully perfected and complete, to the Father – his mission at last accomplished!

This is the context in which we must understand the prayer 'your kingdom come'. The victory of God's kingdom is assured; its sovereignty and power are universal and fully vindicated. But the mop-up operation continues. Satan has been defeated but he does not give up easily, and in spite of his defeat most of the world is still very much under his control. Those who ask how this is possible need only compare it to a situation like that in Iraq, where outside forces won a quick victory in 2003, but have been forced to spend several years trying to bring real peace to that country. Whether they will succeed is doubtful, but their failure serves merely to highlight the contrast between that situation and ours as believers. Unlike the occupying army in Iraq, we are not desperate, because the forces with us are far greater than those ranged against us and there is no possibility of our being defeated and enslaved again.

To apply this practically we must first of all survey the battlefield on which we are called to engage. Where are the pressure points at which the kingdom of God is struggling to make good its victory? The first and greatest is very close to us – it is in the heart of every believer. We have been rescued from Satan's tyranny, but it would be foolish to pretend that we have not been marked by it. After all, his is the only world we have ever known,

---

5. The descent of Jesus Christ into hell is one of the most obscure of
   Christian beliefs, relying as it does on the two witnesses of Eph. 4:9 and
   1 Pet. 3:18. But in a sense this does not matter, because even by coming
   into our world, the Son of God was entering the kingdom of darkness,
   and the main principles outlined here still apply.

and even after our deliverance we continue to live in it. Now that we are Christians, we have become collaborators with Satan's enemy and are therefore prime targets for retribution. Nowhere does the battle for God's kingdom rage more fiercely than inside those who have been called to join it. Every day of our lives, every moment of our conscious existence, we are at war with the devil whether we recognize it or not. Sometimes we let our guard slip and for a while it seems as though the fury of battle has abated. After all, why should Satan waste his strength on those whom he has brought once more under his control? But peace of this kind is an illusion. Hidden in us and perhaps ignored for a time is the presence of God's Holy Spirit, who reveals himself at the moment of his choosing and rises to the struggle once again. By then we may be deep inside enemy territory, unaware of how far we still have to go if we are ever to return to our own side, but this is a small thing in the eyes of God. He can and will reach as far as he has to in order to bring us back to where we should be, and it is often when we are plunged into the depths of despair, with enemy forces surrounding us on every side, that the power of Christ's victory becomes most evident. Those who have been forgiven much love much, but those who have been forgiven little love little (Luke 7:47).

Of course it would be silly, and even blasphemous, to encourage people to sin so that when they finally repent they will get a greater reward (cf. Rom. 6:1). Yet for those who have sinned in ways they think are quite unforgivable, the message of Christ's redeeming love is clear: the further God has to go to rescue you, the more you will love him when he does, and the more secure will be the presence of his kingdom in your heart. That is the consolation he brings, and when Satan reminds us of how bad we really are, that is the assurance we have from God that we shall never again be allowed to sink back into the depths of our former way of life.

The presence of the king

'Your kingdom come.' The presence of the kingdom is inconceivable without the presence of the king. An earthly monarch can be

in only one place at a time. Our own queen is a great traveller and
does her best to visit her far-flung realms and territories as much
as she can, but even she can only come our way every so often. She
does what she is called to do and does it well, but she always acts
within the limits of the constitutional conventions to which she is
subject just as we are. Few of her subjects ever meet her and even
fewer can claim to know her personally. How very different it is
with our heavenly King Jesus! Not only does he visit us, his far-
flung outposts on earth; he actually dwells in us all the time. We
have direct access to him, he hears our prayers and he attends personally to our every need. Yet still we have to pray for his kingdom
to come – why? Present though he is in and among us, our king
does not rule in our lives to the degree he should. The fault is not
his of course, but ours. As the Sovereign Lord of all creation, he
could simply walk into our lives and take them over, but that is
not his way. He has not called us to be his servants, but to be his
brothers and sisters, reigning with him in his kingdom.

For this to work, we have to be willing recipients of his grace.
He stands at the door of our lives and knocks, but unless we open
that door he will not come in and dwell with us in the way he longs
to do. Why do we not open the door to him? Frankly, the main
reason is that we have a secret longing to return to the kingdom of
Satan, however much we may deny it. That is where our roots are,
after all, not to mention so many of our friends, relatives and
neighbours. To put it crudely, the devil we know is often a more
comfortable figure than the God we do not know, or do not know
as deeply as we should. Why go into battle for him when we can
spend our time relaxing in the enemy camp? Why stand out for
him when it is so much easier to put on camouflage and live like
everyone else, keeping our little secret to ourselves? And just look
at the Lord's army – not many wise, not many rich, for God has
chosen the foolish things of this world (1 Cor. 1:26–28), and who
wants to be seen with them? These feelings go very deep, and are
perhaps nowhere more apparent than in those who are called to
high rank in God's forces. It is a terrible thing to say, but the battle-
ground on which we operate is littered with the corpses of biblical
scholars, bishops and ordained ministers of the gospel who have
preferred the praise and glory of this world to the suffering that

would afflict them if they stayed with the people of God. Not only
that, but some of these poor folk have turned on their braver
comrades and attacked them instead of the enemy, calling them
'fundamentalists' or other pejorative things and assuring anyone
who will listen that they want to have nothing to do with such
people. It is a pathetic sight, but ridicule and persecution in the
world are part of the price a faithful witness must pay, and how
many of us are really prepared to pay it? Even when the Holy
Spirit comes into our hearts crying 'Abba, Father!', the old Adam
inside us fights back as hard as he can, and it is only by the grace of
God at work in us that we can find the strength we need to with-
stand and overcome his resistance.

But whatever difficulties we face, we must remain firm and
insist that there can be no coming of the kingdom without the
coming of the king. Whether he comes in humility riding on a
donkey, or in majesty on the clouds of heaven, makes little
difference – it is the presence of the king that transforms everything.[6] Take that away and we are left with nothing. Christmas has
now degenerated into a tawdry commercial festival, but as
Christians we are called to remember what its real message is –
Emmanuel, God with us, the presence of Light in the world (Isa.
7:14; John 1:4–9). Nowadays it is little regarded, but there is a per-
sistent strain of devotion that runs through the history of the
church, in which believers are challenged to reflect whether their
hearts are like the inn at Bethlehem – too full to accommodate the
King of kings. One of the most beautiful expressions of this
devotional tradition comes from the pen of John Donne, the great
metaphysical poet who was also dean of St Paul's Cathedral in
London. Writing on the theme of the incarnation, Donne had this
to say (addressed to the Virgin Mary):

> Immensity cloister'd in thy dear womb,
> Now leaves his well-beloved imprisonment,
> Here he hath made himself to his intent

---

6. The allusions here are to Palm Sunday (Matt. 21:1–11) and to the future
   return of Christ (Matt. 24:30).

Weak enough, now into our world to come;
But oh, for thee, for Him, hath th'Inn no room?

'Hath th'Inn no room?' If we are honest with ourselves, we
shall admit that we resist the coming of the king, because if he
enters our house we shall have to make room for him and that
means giving the house a thorough clean. We do not have to do
this ourselves – he does it for us, but it is painful nevertheless.
Recently, I moved house and found things I never knew I had,
including things that I suspect did not belong to me but had been
left behind by the previous occupants. I had never noticed them,
hidden away in odd corners as they were. But out they had to go,
and when I went into my new place a different arrangement had to
be made to accommodate my possessions. That in turn led to
throwing out even more things, because there simply was not
enough room for them all. If someone else were ever to come and
live in the house, even more would have to go, and I am not sure
that I could bear to part with the stuff I have got – at least not yet.

So it is in the Christian life. We want God to come into our
house, at least in theory, but we are not so prepared for the
upheaval inside that his coming will inevitably bring. We want to
hang on to things we do not need, even to things that may be
harmful and come between us and our Lord. So often we think it
is enough to declare our allegiance to Christ but to deal with him
by post or e-mail, rather than have him with us in the house where
he would be sure to inhibit our freedom and cramp our lifestyle.
But Jesus cannot come into our lives without bringing his kingdom
with him – the two are inseparable. He cannot occupy a room that
has our furniture and possessions in it, because he has brought his
own along with him and we have to make room for them. And so
different are they from the things we already have that we must
throw them out because they look out of place next to what he
brings with him. The only logical thing to do is to let him take over
completely; but how hard it is for us to get to that point. Say what
you like, in the end, our resistance has to be beaten back one step
at a time until his kingdom really does come into our lives.

To understand how this works, we have to realize that the
kingdom of God is not an abstract power that operates on us

from the outside, but a personal relationship with God in Christ sealed by the indwelling presence of his Holy Spirit in our hearts. Some human activities are clearly incompatible with that relationship, and when Jesus comes into our lives they have to go, more or less automatically. For example, nobody would suggest that a prostitute or a professional thief could simply carry on doing those things after coming to Christ, as if nothing had happened, and in those cases it is obvious that the previous life must come to an end when a person is converted. However, it must also be admitted that few cases are as clear-cut as that, since not many people engage in activities unambiguously wrong in themselves. For most of us, the task is much more subtle and difficult. Usually we have to decide whether something we are doing, which might be perfectly legitimate in itself, is unhelpful to my Christian calling and therefore ought to be abandoned.

This can get surprisingly complicated. I once ran a little shop where I was expected to stock pornographic magazines. I refused to do so, and fortunately, my stand was respected by my superiors and I got away with it. But what about daily newspapers, many of which are almost as bad? What about cigarettes and other tobacco products that can be very profitable but harmful to people's health? Where do we draw the line, particularly if we are employed by people who do not share our sensitivities in such matters? None of this affected me directly, of course. I did not read the dubious papers and I did not smoke. When the opportunity arose, I did what I could to discourage others from doing these things as much as I could, but I could not ban them outright. Was I being a witness for the truth in a dark world, or was I compromising myself by indirectly fostering activities I knew to be wrong? There is no easy answer to questions like these, and in our fallen world we must expect that different people will come to different conclusions. Some will take a strict line and insist that no-one should ever be a party to the undesirable behaviour of others, though consistency in this respect is extremely difficult to achieve. Others will adopt a 'lesser of two evils' approach and compromise to some extent, while trying to keep as 'clean' as possible themselves. There can be no absolute right or wrong here, and each individual must be guided by his or her own conscience in the light of prevailing circumstances.

This is especially true of political life. Nobody can engage in democratic politics without being compromised in some way or other, because that is the nature of democracy. Those who refuse to bend eventually find themselves on the lunatic fringe in the company of other similarly rigid people, whose particular causes may be very far removed from anything we would want to be associated with. One of the odder things about the European Parliament is that British members who have got themselves elected on an anti-European platform, which they advocate in the name of greater democracy, have found themselves seated next to neo-fascist groups from other countries, who are also opposed to the European idea, though for completely different reasons. Is this the sort of witness Christians want to be? Sticking to our guns can lead to some odd alliances, which may or may not be tolerable. Yet for believers to back off altogether and leave politics to those who do not share our principles is hardly a valid option, since we are called to be the salt of the earth and the light of the world (Matt. 5:13–16). Christians who do not get involved in politics themselves still want to be able to vote for others who agree with their fundamental principles. They demonstrate by this that they expect there to be a Christian presence in government, even if it is not always the dominant voice.

When we turn from essentially external things to what we think, say and do in our private lives, decisions can become even harder. For example, I was brought up believing it was sensible and frugal to steam unfranked postage stamps off envelopes and reuse them, and I still remember the sense of shock I felt when I eventually realized that this was a form of stealing. Does God really care about the odd postage stamp? Does the post office? It all seems so trivial, but life is made up of such trivialities, and when our consciences are pricked by such apparently small matters, we have to obey them. What do we do about beggars in the street who ask us for money? People who know about such things understand that, in Western countries at least, most of these people have no need to beg and may be part of criminal gangs that prey on tender consciences to make money. Giving to them is rather like feeding pigeons in the park – tempting at the time but not a good idea in the long run. But can we pass by such people without feeling like the Pharisee and the Levite in the story of the good Samaritan, who were too busy and too self-righteous to help someone in genuine need (Luke 10:25–37)?

Here there is a particular problem faced by those in full-time Christian ministry, who are often expected to show compassion in such circumstances, however naive and unhelpful it may actually be. When the choice is between being called a hypocrite by those asking for help and a fool by those who understand what is really going on, what is the right decision to take? Will one answer fit all situations, or are we forced to move forward by a process of trial and error, leaning sometimes one way and sometimes the other? Again, ministers of the gospel may have to read books or watch films they would never recommend to others, but cannot advise against if they do not know what they are. Straightforward pornography may be easy enough to avoid, but what about films like *The Last Temptation of Christ*? What about books like *The Da Vinci Code*, or *The God Delusion*? Can I read such things, even as a critic, without being marked in some way by them? How do I decide what to pick up and what to leave on the shelf? How conscious must I be that my behaviour in this regard may have a negative effect on others, who expect me to lead by example?

What happens when private affections clash with public principles that must be upheld in the church? It often happens that relatives of ours do things we know are wrong, but to what extent are we prepared to put principle before family ties and obligations? Should Christian parents turn a blind eye if one of their children decides to cohabit with someone else instead of getting married? Whose side do we take in the case of divorce? Will a principled response lead to a change of heart on the part of the offenders, or will it merely drive them into permanent alienation, not only from the family but from God and the church as well? And what do we do when someone close to us falls into some form of liberal theology, which is the intellectual equivalent of committing adultery? Does 'loving the sinner' in this case mean allowing him to preach or teach in the church? One would think not, but anybody who has tried to exercise spiritual discipline in such cases will know how difficult it can be to go against powerful social ties and expectations.

More subtle still is the whole realm of thoughts and attitudes, which many of us do not even think to tackle. To what extent are our views shaped by personal preferences that amount in practice to little more than irrational prejudice, which we nevertheless ascribe to Christian conviction? We may believe that sinners can be forgiven in theory, but are we prepared to do it in practice, particularly when the sin in question is a decidedly antisocial one? Sometimes people commit youthful indiscretions and end up paying a heavy price, if (for example) they are placed on a sex-offenders register for the rest of their lives. How far would we be prepared to resist popular antagonism in helping them to return to a normal life, perhaps by recommending them for potentially controversial types of employment? And what about the extraordinary prejudice against single people in ministry, which is all but universal in the Protestant world? We may rightly reject the Roman Catholic insistence on clerical celibacy, but do we then go to the opposite extreme and push people into unsuitable marriages, simply in order to give them a job? Do we realize, when we think like this, that neither Jesus nor the apostle Paul would be welcome in most of our churches, simply because they were not married? Do we believe what the apostle Paul says in 1 Corinthians 7, or do we simply expend all the hermeneutical ingenuity we can muster to nullify the clear implications of his teaching because it does not chime in with our own deep-seated prejudices? Dozens of other similar examples could be mentioned, but the point must surely be clear by now. The kingdom of God has a long way to go if it is ever to take root in our hearts as it should, indeed as it must, if we are ever to become the children of God and witnesses to the gospel that he has called us to be.

Your will be done[7]

God's kingdom comes when his will, and not ours, is done in our lives. But once again, what seems to be fairly straightforward and

---

7. Neither this nor the following phrase is found in Luke's version of the prayer, but both are fully consistent with the teaching of Jesus found elsewhere.

obvious in theory often turns out to be a tall order in practice. The battlefield on which we are called to fight for Christ is strewn with landmines that have to be detected and rooted out, and no land-mine is more dangerous than the one lodged deep inside our will. It is often thought that the will is part of the higher element in human nature, part indeed of the image of God in us. Down through the ages, eminent theologians have insisted that our will is free, and that as human beings, we can and must be able to choose whether to submit to God or not. Any notion that God might somehow be controlling our will is rejected by these people as dehumanizing and therefore unworthy of God, who (as they insist) wants us to make up our own minds. Yet the truth of the matter is that the will is not a function of God's image in us or a spark of the divine. It is a function of our human nature and, because of that, it responds instinctively to what the Bible calls the 'flesh'. This is not something that has come about because of the fall of Adam. It was so even in the Garden of Eden, since it was Adam's will, responding to the temptation of the flesh, that led him into sin in the first place.

Even Jesus knew the force of this, because in the Garden of Gethsemane, on the night he was betrayed, he prayed to the Father: 'Not my will, but your will be done' (Luke 22:42). How can this be? If the Father and the Son are both God and there is only one God, why do they not have the same will? How can Jesus imply not only that his will is distinct from the Father's, but (in this case at least) is apparently contradictory to it? The answer is that because the will is a function of nature, Jesus had two wills, just as he had two natures – one divine and the other human. In his divine will he was one with the Father, because there is only one divine nature uniting all three persons of the Godhead. But in his human nature he had another will, and this will was bound to the flesh, whose desires it expressed. Jesus the Son of God went to his death voluntarily, but Jesus the human being could not willingly accept his own extinction. The instinct for self-preservation is basic to our human nature, and had Jesus shown no sign of this he would not have been fully human. In Gethsemane, it was this human will that was asserting itself, as it had to if Jesus was a psy-chologically normal human being and not some masochistic creature gone mad. In telling the Father that he did not want to die, Jesus was not rebelling against his Father's will. On the contrary, he was revealing how deep and how all-embracing the call of obedience to that will must be. As the writer to the Hebrews put it, the Son of Man learned obedience through what he suffered, because had he not done so, he could not have become our Saviour (Heb. 5:8–9). That his human will was contrary to the divine will is only to be expected, because human and divine nature are different and essentially incompatible. What happened in Gethsemane was not some kind of conjunction of the wills, not a co-operation of the human with the divine in order to achieve God's purpose, but rather a *surrender* of the human will to the divine one. Even in Jesus, the desires of the flesh had to be mortified, and no desire is more universal or fundamental than the desire for survival. Only when that was put to death could he go to his death on the cross, because only then would the latter take effect as something truly voluntary on his part.

It is a myth to suppose that human beings have free will in any spiritual sense. As in the case of Jesus, our will is a function of our human nature and acts in accordance with it. That nature is not necessarily evil, but is self-interested and the will acts accordingly. Its most basic manifestation is the instinct for survival, which is essentially a good thing, but it can appear in many other guises as well, some of which are far less admirable. The drive for success, for example, may have laudable aspects to it, but it may also be the gateway to corruption and crime. But whether it is directed towards fair ends or foul ones, our human will is bound by our finite nature and for that reason it cannot even begin to understand the will of God. For that to happen, God must intervene in my life and make his will known to me. When he does this, the result is a spiritual crisis. It has to be like that, because when I become aware of God's will I also become aware that I am not doing it. Accompanying this is the further awareness that without his help I cannot do it, even if I want to. The only solution is repentance and submission to his will, something made possible for me by his Holy Spirit at work in my heart.

There are many learned and godly pastors who interpret Paul's account of his spiritual struggle with the will in Romans 7 as properly belonging to his pre-conversion days, although it has to be said that this flies in the face of both the plain meaning of the text and of everyday experience. People who are not Christians and who have no idea of what God's will might be are not bothered by it; doing God's will is not a problem for them because they have never had to face it. Only when God gets to work in our lives do we start to become aware of the difficulty, because only then do we begin to consider God's will at all. The plain fact of the matter is that anyone trying to live the Christian life knows full well that his will is at odds with God's, and that human strength alone is not enough to put this right. For believers, every day brings a renewed struggle for submission – your will be done! To claim that this problem disappears at conversion is to go against the facts of experience, and I believe that great harm has been done, however unintentionally, by this misinterpretation of the apostle Paul. To be bothered about our own spiritual inadequacies is the mark of the Christian, not of the unbeliever, because it is God's way of telling us that we must turn to him for help. If we cease to be reminded of this, it is almost certainly because we have fallen away from him and are no longer listening to his voice.

The closer we get to God and the nearer his kingdom comes in our hearts, the greater the struggle will be. Anyone who has ever gone on a diet will understand this. The first few pounds come off in a day or two and for a while everything seems to be going according to plan. Then you hit a plateau and for a long time nothing seems to be happening at all. You may even lose ground at some point and fall back to an earlier stage. Finally you start to pick up again, but losing those last ten pounds is the hardest of all. The nearer you come to the goal the harder it gets and the more self-discipline it demands. It is exactly the same in the spiritual life. Obeying God is easy at the beginning, in the first enthusiasm of a newly converted life. Nothing seems to be too difficult or too demanding to be sacrificed for him. But after a while the initial euphoria wears off, the going gets tougher and we begin to wonder whether we shall ever make any progress at all. We may even backslide for a time, despairing of any real progress. Then slowly but surely, God reveals how he has been at work on us, reaching into parts of our lives of which we have no conscious awareness, changing and preparing us for the next stage of our growth. But when that comes we start to realize just how hard the going can be. Cleaning out the hidden corners of our lives, surrendering the obscurer parts of our will to God's sovereign power – these things are difficult and demanding. Nobody notices them in the way they notice the enthusiasm of a new Christian. Very often our secret sins are so embarrassing even to ourselves that we would not dare to share them with anyone else, nor does God expect us to do that. What he wants is to conquer ever more parts of our lives, to subdue us and to shape us into instruments for his glory and for the spread of his kingdom in the world. 'Your will be done' is a prayer for change in our lives so that there may be change in the world – the one flows inexorably from the other.

If there is one thing we have learned in the past hundred years, it is that trying to change the world without changing the people in it is a hopeless enterprise. Yet everywhere we turn that is precisely what we find. Huge campaigns are launched and spend billions of dollars to bring change to the dark corners of the earth. These activities are more or less well intentioned, of course, and we should not despise or underestimate that. But all of them are wasted without the inner spiritual change that alone can make it work. Giving a sinner a million dollars merely increases his opportunities to sin, as anyone who has tried it will tell you.

Some years ago I was part of a project to raise money for the rebuilding of a theological college in Uganda, which had been devastated by civil war in that country in the early 1980s. We collected thousands of pounds and sent skilled volunteers to the site to help with the rebuilding, only to find that the local bishop had spent the money on a Mercedes and nothing at all had been done to rebuild the college! The arrival of skilled labour from abroad quickly transformed the situation, but only for a time. We spent days laying pipes for running water and were about to turn on the tap and start the flow when we discovered that the men who had been putting the pipes down by day were digging them up at night, because they thought they could do better by selling the lead and pocketing the cash. We thought we were helping them, only to discover that they preferred to help themselves! What I observed in a single village is a picture of what is happening all over the world, sometimes on a scale that defies the imagination. Providing the means to achieve great things is never enough by itself; hearts and minds have to be submitted to the will of God if any of this provision is to bear fruit in the way it should.

One of the most difficult aspects of this prayer is the need to accept God's will, even when it turns out to be something quite different from what we have imagined. Nobody has a problem if God happens to agree with them and they get what they ask for. It is only when this does not happen that our faith is put to the test, and sadly, many people fail to pass it. Seen from a distance, the story of a woman who prayed unsuccessfully that her elderly mother would be allowed to live and not be taken away by illness may seem to be somewhat unrealistic – after all, we all have to die sometime. But few of us can be that detached when the matter comes close to home. Things are made even worse when people convince themselves that all they have to do is pray and God will give them the 'right' answer. Hard as it is to believe, there are people who have been so convinced of this that they have sold their possessions, travelled across the world and cut off any avenue of escape, all because they have been totally convinced that a particular course of action is the one God has mapped out for them. To their minds, taking precautions and keeping other options open may even appear to be a sign of lack of faith, because if God has revealed his will to them, to do anything other than conform to it is an indication of unbelief. Dealing with people of that kind is never easy, and when their delusions are shattered, the fallout can be disastrous. It is not for others to judge, but we must at least wonder whether the 'faith' they claimed to profess and that was so clearly charted out for them, was really genuine.

The apostle Paul tells us that 'we walk by faith, not by sight' (2 Cor. 5:7). Many people interpret this to mean that we can never be sure what is going on, and in extreme cases it can be used as an excuse to justify a fatalistic approach to life. As the Italians say, *che serà, serà* – whatever will be, will be. There may be some elementary human wisdom in that, but it is not what the apostle teaches. Nor has it ever been Christian doctrine to say that we are puppets in the hands of some inexorable fate. The difference between walking by faith and walking by sight can be most readily appreciated by looking at the object in view. Those who walk by sight have a clear vision of where they are headed; whatever obstacles they may encounter along the way, they are sure they will get there in the end. People who interpret God's will in terms of a particular course of action that will not fail to bring results may claim to be walking by faith, but in fact have turned their faith into sight and are heading straight towards that goal. The possibility that God might have some other plan never crosses their mind, and if things do not work out as expected, they may be so shaken that they lose the faith they claim to have.

To walk by faith in the true sense is a different experience altogether. True faith is more than just a set of beliefs. It is primarily a relationship with God in and through Jesus Christ, whom we trust to know what is best for us and to work it out in our lives in the time and way most necessary for us. When we think in these terms, the precise details cease to matter because we know that the One who is watching over us will guide and protect us whatever might happen along the way to our final destination. The psalmist expressed it most beautifully when he wrote:

> Even though I walk through the valley of the shadow of death,
>   I will fear no evil,
> for you are with me;
>   your rod and your staff,
>   they comfort me.
> (Ps. 23:4)

These words have become some of the most famous in the entire Bible, not so much because they are well written or poetically stated as because they bear witness to a truth that has echoed through the lives of generations of faithful believers. The valley of the shadow of death is a place of darkness and uncertainty, far removed from the world of those who walk by sight, yet it holds no terrors for those who trust in Christ. The rod and the staff are ambiguous – they may be gentle reminders of where the right way lies, but they may also be uncomfortable rebukes to those who have gone astray. Either way, though, their presence is a comfort, because it reminds us that God cares for us and keeps us headed in the right direction.

As I look back over my own life I can say that there have been many times when the future has been far from clear. There have been occasions in my life when I have had no job, no money and no roof over my head – and no immediate prospect of getting any of these. I have often had good cause to wonder what tomorrow will bring and little objective evidence that it would be anything positive. The only thing I can say for sure is that if I had planned my life to follow a particular pattern I would have packed it all in long ago, since the one consistently recurring phenomenon is that I have never yet got any of the jobs I have applied for! But that is far from being the whole story. However dark the valley of the shadow of death through which I have had to walk may have been, it has never put out the light of faith. Even in the hardest places, I have felt the rod and the staff of God's protecting love reaching out to me and giving me hope for the future. What is more, that hope has been rewarded time and time again. Doors I did not know existed have opened up, opportunities of which I could never have dreamed have unexpectedly come my way. I have never been abandoned and, to tell the truth, have never seriously thought I would be. By having my own will denied, I have been set free to wait eagerly for the revelation of God's will in my life, and the wonderful thing is that his will has always turned out to be something far better than anything I could have imagined by myself. Submitting to God's will, allowing it to come in and take over your future, is never settling for second best. When God gets to work in our lives, it is to do things we could never have dreamed of, and to do them in ways of which we would not have been capable on our own, if only because we would never have thought of them.

Is this really true? Have I made it up, by interpreting perfectly ordinary events in a way that suits my own predilection for the miraculous and spectacular? No doubt there are many sceptics who will say that that is exactly what I have done. Indeed, their ignorance of both God and his will leaves them with little choice but to say that. There is a wonderful story told about the late Archbishop Donald Coggan, who was once asked how he knew that what he regarded as 'answers to prayer' were not just coincidences which would have happened anyway, whether he had

prayed about them or not. Dr Coggan replied that although that
might be so, he had noticed that when he stopped praying, the
coincidences stopped happening! Those who walk by faith understand what the archbishop was saying because they recognize it
from their own experience. More than doctrine, more than
worship, more than church structures, it is this common experience of faith that binds Christians together and helps us to know
when we are walking with fellow sheep and when we have fallen
among a herd of goats. 'Your will be done' is the authentic voice
of Christians who know in their hearts and have learned from
experience that there is no better way to ensure that one day we
shall pass through the valley of the shadow of death and cross
over to the glorious courts of the kingdom when it finally comes
to dwell in us for ever.

Before we leave this theme and move on, we must return briefly
to what we noticed at the beginning of this section. There are
only two places in the Bible where the phrase 'your will be done'
occurs – here, and on the lips of Jesus in the Garden of
Gethsemane. It seems most unlikely that the use of the same
phrase in two such central New Testament passages, and nowhere
else, can have been an accident. Jesus is the only biblical figure
recorded as having prayed this way, even though we could argue
that he was also the only one who did not have to do so! The last
great prayer of his earthly ministry was clearly putting into practice the teaching he gave his disciples, and in that act of obedience
we find the consistency between word and deed we would expect
of him. But is it possible to look at this the other way round, and
suggest that in giving this word to his disciples to form part of
their prayer, Jesus was drawing them, and through them us, into a
deeper understanding of and participation in his own suffering
and death for our redemption? When we pray 'your will be done'
are we in some mysterious way being put next to him in
Gethsemane and being allowed to share in that central moment of
his life?

In suggesting this, we must be careful to avoid the misunder-
standings that can so easily arise. We are not saying that we
co-operate in the work of our own salvation, which is entirely his
work on our behalf. Nothing we say or do can add to or detract

from that work which he accomplished for us, once and for all, on the cross. Nor are we suggesting that our relationship with God has anything like the depth the Son's relationship has with the Father. What passed between them in the garden touches a level of divine love that is revealed to us but that we can never truly share, because we are not Persons of the Godhead ourselves. We must be humble here, and not try to intrude on a relationship that passes all human understanding.

But having said that, there are times in the New Testament when we are told that as Christians we are privileged to share in some mysterious way in the sufferings and death of the Lord Jesus. The experience of conversion is a case in point. Only one conversion is described in detail in the Bible, but what a conversion it is. Saul of Tarsus was a man who hated the church to the point of persecuting it, a man who was so sure he knew God's will for his life – another case of walking by sight and mistaking it for faith – that it never occurred to him to ask whether he was right or not. It was that man who was struck blind by the light of Christ who appeared to him on the road to Damascus (Acts 9:1–19). But look at the details. Is it an accident that Saul remained in his blinded state for three days, the same amount of time that Jesus spent in the tomb? Is it merely a coincidence that during that time he neither ate nor drank anything, as if he were indeed dead and buried? And why is it that when he got up from the ground after seeing the vision, the word Luke used is not the normal one for getting up off the ground, but the one used to describe the resurrection of Jesus? We cannot press the comparison too far of course, but the echoes of Christ's death and resurrection are there for those who have ears to hear. Furthermore, since the New Testament tells us so often that as Christians we are privileged to share in Christ's sufferings, it seems impossible to escape the conclusion that our prayers must also reflect something of his great prayer at the moment of his passion (2 Cor. 1:5–7; Phil. 3:10; 1 Pet. 4:13).

To pray for God's will to be done in our lives is to pray for a deeper union with Christ in his suffering, death and resurrection. It is here that God's will and the coming of the kingdom meet. Christ the king stands in relation to his kingdom as the head stands in

relation to the body, and we are the body of Christ (1 Cor. 12:12)!
Modern Christians have become accustomed to hearing the church
referred to as Christ's body, though all too often this seems to
happen in contexts that appear to be justifying administrative cen-
tralization and the increased concentration of ecclesiastical power
in a few bureaucratic hands. Needless to say, the New Testament
paints a rather different picture. There the body of Christ is not the
glorious throng of thousands paying homage to some earthly representative of the head, but the bread that is broken to remind us
of the sacrifice he made for us on the cross. The unity we have is
the work of the Holy Spirit, binding together any number of dis-
parate and apparently contradictory elements, and transforming
them in the process – by breaking them and then building them
afresh from scratch. There can be no greater glory than to be so
closely tied to Christ that we can say with the apostle Paul that we
are 'filling up what is lacking in Christ's afflictions for the sake of
his body' (Col. 1:24). Since there cannot have been anything lacking
in Christ's afflictions, it is clear that this can mean only that the
Saviour has permitted the apostle to bear something of his own
burden, rather in the way parents will sometimes let a child 'help' in
some domestic chore while in reality doing the work themself!

To pray 'your will be done' is to pray that we shall be so close to
Christ that we shall no longer notice the difference between his
burden and ours, when we shall see our sufferings as part of his
and come to understand that because they are his, our sufferings
have been eternally redeemed by him.

On earth as it is in heaven

The Lord's prayer assumes that God's will is already being done in
heaven, and implies that what is happening there is the pattern
which we should be praying to see established on earth. It may
seem strange that we should be asked to think about heaven a
second time in as many lines, but the logic behind this is clear. In
the first line, we were asked to consider the spiritual significance of
'heaven' as God's dwelling-place, whereas now we are being challenged to think about what that means in relation to the world we
live in, and what practical impact it has on us.

The language used here recalls the narrative of creation in Genesis 1: 'In the beginning, God created the heavens and the earth' (Gen. 1:1). In Genesis, heaven and earth are both regarded as parts of God's creation, which have been ordered in a way that allows them to complement and interact with one other. The sun, moon and stars govern the physical heavens and give light to the earth, while the waters above 'the firmament', to use the lovely biblical phrase, send their rain down to water the crops. Without this heaven to support us, life on earth would be impossible. The physical meanings of the words 'heaven' and 'earth' illustrate the spiritual ones, and this line of the Lord's Prayer provides us with a clear link between them. The spiritual sense of the word 'earth' is clearly related to that of the 'world', which is the domain of Satan, but there is a subtle difference between the two terms that comes out most clearly in the different ways in which the adjectives 'earthly' and 'worldly' are used. To be 'worldly' is to have the mind of Satan, the prince of this world, whereas to be 'earthly' is simply to be bound by the horizons of this finite universe. As children of Adam, who was taken from the earth, we are all 'earthly' by nature and cannot escape this condition as long as we remain in this life. But this does not mean we have to be 'worldly' in our thinking. The presence of the Holy Spirit in our lives strengthens and supplements the defects of what is 'earthly', but takes away what is 'worldly' entirely. Nevertheless, we must bear in mind that the earthly and the worldly are sufficiently similar to one another as to make the one susceptible of falling into the clutches of the other. As Christians we have been delivered from the spiritual power of the world but are still capable of being tempted by it, and even of falling back into it, because our earthly natures have not yet been fully overcome.

In spiritual terms, then, we can say that heaven is a state of order, where God's will is done, earth is a state of weakness where God's will struggles against opposition, and the world is a state of rebellion that has fallen completely under the control of Satan. It is possible for God's will to be done on earth but not in the 'world', because if that were to happen, the 'world' would cease to exist. There has always been a temptation in the Christian church to conclude that the physical earth is the 'world', which has led to the widespread belief that anyone seeking to escape from Satan's rebellion must try to get as far away from the finite universe as possible and live in a way that consciously anticipates the coming of the kingdom of heaven. The intention is a good one, of course, but because the assumptions on which it rests are false, the result is a caricature of the truth that is at best ridiculous and at worst harmful to our spiritual growth.

Let me take a concrete example of this to illustrate what I mean. For many centuries it has been thought that because there is no marriage in heaven (Mark 12:25), spiritually minded people should prepare themselves for this by not marrying on earth either. In the Roman Catholic Church this belief has been institutionalized to the point where celibacy is imposed on all officially 'religious' people.[8] Other Christians reject this interpretation as being too extreme, but rather than simply dismiss it, we ought to try to understand what motivates it and explain why we think it is wrong. Clerical celibacy was originally intended to give the church a living witness of how God's will can be done on earth as it is done in heaven. Rome has always recognized that such self-discipline is beyond the power of the average Christian, but it wants a picture of the ideal to stand before the people as a reminder of the heavenly destiny God intends for us. From the Protestant point of view, the mistake with this is to assume that obedience to the will of God on earth is best secured by a literal imitation of heaven, at least to the extent that such a thing is possible. In response to this,

---

8. In the Roman Catholic Church, the word 'religious' has a technical sense, used of monks and nuns, who live according to a set of rules known as a 'religion'. The opposite to this is 'secular', another technical term used mainly of ordained clergy who are not monks. The lines between them were crossed in 1123, when the first Lateran council mandated celibacy, traditionally a 'religious' discipline, for the 'secular' clergy as well, a situation that has continued to the present. The Eastern Orthodox churches have not followed this development, and confine celibacy to the 'religious'. Their bishops have to be celibate, but this is because they must be drawn from the ranks of the monks and not from the 'secular' clergy. No Protestant church imposes this rule on any of its clergy.

we say that we have no quarrel with the celibate angels who do the will of God in heaven, but we also insist that we are not angels, nor are we meant to become like them here on earth. Our circumstances are different from theirs and the commands of God given to us are different also. As human beings dwelling on the physical earth we are commanded to be part of that earth and to follow its norms of procreation unless God has set us apart for some special purpose that makes it better for us to remain celibate. As the apostle Paul demonstrated, that is a real possibility and we must admit that many Protestants are reluctant (to put it mildly) to admit this. But however desirable it may be, celibacy remains the exception rather than the rule, and to force it on everyone who is ordained is to go well beyond anything commanded in Scripture.

At the same time, we must also recognize that marriage is for this earthly life only, and that when we get to heaven we shall be as celibate as the angels are now (Matt. 22:30). But to say that matrimony is not made in or for heaven is not to deny that there is a right way to follow the divine command to 'be fruitful and multiply and fill the earth', which we must respect (Gen. 1:28). The Bible makes it clear from the story of Adam and Eve that heterosexual monogamy is God's way of choice for us, and we must do our best to practise this ideal in our own lives. We are not perfect people, and failures will certainly occur, but the fundamental principle must never be lost sight of. It is hard for modern people to accept it, but it is for this reason that polygamy (which traditionally Christian societies still forbid) is a more tolerable option in God's eyes than homosexuality, which has recently been decriminalized and legalized to varying degrees in the Western world. The reason for the Bible's apparent laxity towards the former but strictness with respect to the latter is because, for all its faults, polygamy at least remains within the laws of creation. There have even been times in human history when it has seemed to be the only way in which the creation mandate could be properly executed, as in the case of Abraham whose wife Sarah was unable to have children. It was Sarah herself who told Abraham to sleep with her handmaid Hagar, because she understood that someone had to provide the children Abraham needed if his name was to survive into future generations (Gen. 16:1–3). It was not a happy

arrangement and, as Sarah was later to discover, it was not
God's solution to the problem of finding an heir for Abraham.
But nobody in this extraordinary story was criticized for practising polygamy (or concubinage) as such. Later it became quite
common.

Jacob had two wives and two concubines who gave birth to his
twelve sons. Elkanah, the father of Samuel, also had two wives,
apparently without any adverse comment from anyone. David and
Solomon may be regarded as record-holders in the field, although
some people have interpreted their well-documented family problems as an indication that God did not approve of their
polygamous behaviour. By New Testament times the pendulum
had swung in the opposite direction. Polygamy had died out
among the Jews, and we know that Jesus had strong objections to
easy divorce, which even his disciples thought were harsh (Matt.
19:1–12). But in spite of this social change, Abraham, Jacob,
David and Solomon were all held up as spiritual predecessors of
Christ and so they have remained in Christian teaching, even
though not one of them would be allowed to hold office in any
church today!

Homosexual practice, on the other hand, was always considered
wrong because it denies the law of creation, turns sexual activity in
on itself and sends the world a message of sterility and death. In a
sense, it can be regarded as a secular equivalent of clerical celibacy,
which may be the reason why it is so attractive to people in the
Catholic tradition who want to avoid procreation but do not want
the loneliness of the single life.

What strikes us today most obviously in the sexual sphere is
present in other dimensions of life as well. There is a long tradition
of monastic asceticism that advocates prolonged fasting, sleepless-
ness and even self-flagellation – all of which are justified as the
'mortification of the flesh' of which the apostle Paul speaks,
although he evidently intended that to be interpreted in a spiritual,
not a literal, sense (Rom. 8:13; Col. 3:5). Most people today think of
such things as somewhat exotic and outside their own experience,
but we must remember that the young Martin Luther was convinced it was by such practices that he would beat the devil out of
his body and become a child of God. It was only when he read in

the Bible that 'the just shall live by faith' and not by such works of piety that he realized what the Christian message was all about – and the Reformation resulted (Rom. 1:17, quoting Hab. 2:4).

The key to seeing the will of God done on earth is not some artificial imitation of the life of heaven, but obedience to the commands of God given to us in this life. These commands are no secret and are readily available to us in his Word, the holy Scriptures. Of course there is a whole army of pundits ready to tell us that things are not that simple. As they like to remind us, a command like 'thou shalt not kill' raises difficult questions about the morality of war against an evil tyrant; 'thou shalt not steal' can hardly apply to a starving man who desperately needs food to survive, and 'thou shalt not commit adultery' imposes a heavy burden on media stars and politicians, who already sacrifice so much of themselves to keep us all entertained and can surely be excused some well-publicized indiscretions as long as they further this aim. In response to this, we have to agree that simple principles almost always have to be worked out in complex situations, and each case must be weighed on its merits. Jesus himself demonstrated that there were times when the law of God had to be broken in the literal sense if it was to be fulfilled in spirit, as when he healed on the Sabbath and also allowed his disciples to gather grain on that day in order to have something to eat (Mark 2:27–28). Obedience to God's commands does not mean we have to be simplistic in the way we work this out, but however complicated things get, we are still expected to be faithful to the principles he has laid down. To give but one obvious example of this, loving my neighbour does not mean it is all right to sleep with him or her, even if that is what the world nowadays so often means when it talks about 'love'. God's command must be applied in ways consistent with the overall tenor of Scripture, and in this case the prohibitions against fornication, adultery and homosexuality must be allowed to control our interpretation and limit the options available to us.

In fact, if we keep the prayer 'your will be done' clearly before our eyes, we shall find that the moral dilemmas that confront us are neither so many nor so intractable as they are often made to appear. Jesus cut through the complex rabbinical regulations that surrounded the working out of the Ten Commandments by going straight to their spiritual heart. For him, 'you shalt not murder' was not an invitation to discuss some form of just war theory, with a view to finding reasons why the command would not apply in certain cases. On the contrary, his teaching was that this command, like the others, was meant to be internalized. Then, as now, very few people committed murder in the criminal sense of the term, and Jesus knew perfectly well that most of his hearers had ticked that particular commandment off in their minds as 'not applicable'. But by telling them that anyone who harbours hatred in his heart towards another person has killed him already, he made an apparently 'safe' bit of the law suddenly relevant to everyone.

Doing God's will on earth as it is done in heaven is just as much of a challenge now as it has ever been. On the subject of 'thou shalt not kill', there has recently been a very good example of this in connection with euthanasia. Liberal groups have been pressing for many years to allow the terminally ill to end their own lives, to give them, as they put it, the 'right to die'. Conservatives have opposed this, partly because it goes against the fundamental law of life but also because it could easily be abused by unscrupulous people wanting others to die for purely selfish reasons, like the promise of an inheritance. Remarkably, at its annual convention in 2006, the British Medical Association (BMA) rejected calls for a liberalization of the law and came out in favour of palliative care for the incurably ill. The BMA is not a Christian organization and would probably not have accepted moral or spiritual arguments against euthanasia if they had been made by theologians or church leaders. What swayed them was the evidence, provided by Christian doctors, that euthanasia was bad medical practice. By following the teaching of the sixth commandment, Christian doctors have been able to find other ways of dealing with the terrible problem of incurable illness, and they have been so successful in alleviating the pain and suffering that such illness causes that their arguments are now regarded as persuasive in the secular medical world. In seeking to do God's will, these Christians have been neither simplistic nor indifferent to suffering, but the very opposite, and the profundity of their approach has been such that it is the liberals who have been made to appear as one-dimensional and uncaring.

This is the kind of obedience Christ demands of us and it is this we pray for when we ask for God's will to be done on earth. A few years ago there was a craze in America that saw millions of people wearing wristbands with the letters WWJD on them. This stands for 'What would Jesus do?' As so often, the intention behind it was a good one – the originators of the fad wanted people to consider how they should take responsible moral decisions when faced with the practical problems of everyday life. Where they went wrong was in assuming that the earthly Jesus should be our model in this respect. Many American evangelicals are teetotal, and institutions controlled by them usually have strict regulations banning alcohol. If Jesus were to come along and start turning water into wine, he would presumably be thrown out for breaking the rules (cf. John 2:1–12)! Does this mean Christians today are justified in flouting such regulations? Is that what Jesus would do if he were to come back to earth today? In these circumstances, the behavioural principle presented to us by WWJD cannot be applied in practice, and a closer examination of Jesus' life will soon show that it is not so much what Jesus did (in particular situations far removed from our lives today) as what he taught that really counts. For this reason, the real question is not 'What would Jesus do?' but 'What does Jesus want me to do?' There is not a double standard at work here – one rule for him and another for the rest of us – but rather a recognition that we are in the world for a different reason. The Son of God came to earth in order to die for our sins, something none of us is called to do. His earthly life and ministry reflected that fact, and for that reason it was in significant respects quite different from the life you and I are called to lead in his service.

We who are Christians are in a different situation to that of the earthly Jesus because we are called to bear witness to the salvation he has already won for us, not to repeat the process in our own lives. Our task is different, and so the ways in which we shall be called to fulfil it are different also. This is not to say I should never curse a fig tree, if that is what God wants me to do for some reason, but I should not assume that just because Jesus did this it is perfectly all right, indeed essential, for me to do the same thing

(Matt. 21:19–20). If that were the case, God's will would be clear
and we would not need to pray about it. But what he wants from us
is not so clear, and at any given moment we must seek his guidance
to know what we should do next. Discerning his will for our lives is
sometimes easy and sometimes very difficult, but the common
denominator, and the one that links us to Jesus himself, is obedience. Obedience is the key to the Christian life at every level.
Before I lay the alternative possibilities before God and ask him to
tell me which one is right for me to follow, I need to make sure I
am willing to obey him in any of the possible ways forward there
may be. Of course, it will probably be the case that when I apply
this criterion, certain options will rule themselves out, because they
do not pass the test. God is unlikely to want me to become a terrorist or a pimp, but although we can be fairly certain of this, we still
have to remember that he asked some of the Old Testament
prophets to do things that would not be widely accepted today. For
example, Ezekiel was told to bake bread on human dung (Ezek.
4:12), and Hosea was ordered to go out and marry a prostitute –
not things that would be widely recommended today (Hos. 1:2).
Even back then, these things were unusual and extraordinary, and
we can hardly claim them as examples of what we should be doing
now when they were not used that way at the time. What we do
have to remember is that God is free to call us to do some strange
things, and if he does, we must be prepared to do them, even if
they go against the accepted norms of modern society or the
official teaching of the church.

The rule for us is that we must actively seek God's will, and
when we know what that is, do it – however costly that may turn
out to be. If we trust and obey his leading, however strange and
incomprehensible it may seem at times, he will honour and reward
our obedience in ways that we could never foresee and we shall
learn all over again what it means to walk in his will all the days of
our life. If we happen to go astray through ignorance or excessive
zeal he will bring us back to the right path and teach us what it
means to put his commands into practice. This is what Jesus wants
us to do – and what he would do, if he were in our shoes.

3. GIVE US THIS DAY OUR DAILY BREAD

The demands of the Christian lifestyle

In the third petition of the Lord's Prayer we move from the praise and adoration of God to intercession. As we stop to think about it, which we seldom do, it may come as a surprise to discover just how blunt and basic that intercession is. Those of us who were well brought up know that we do not ask for things without saying 'please', but there is no sign of that here. This is not because Jesus wants us to be ill mannered or rude, but because he wants us to appreciate just how desperate we are. The beggar in the street does not have time for the niceties of middle-class politeness, and it is he who is our closest model when we stand before God. We are not talking here about choices or preferences, about things we could just as easily do without, but about the most fundamental necessities of existence. It is a matter of basic survival, of life and death. 'Give us this day our daily bread' touches the most basic level of our being, and because it reaches down as deep as it is possible to go, it includes every dimension of our need. There is nothing we can provide for ourselves: it all comes from God. If he were to stop sending the rain, if he were to burn the earth to a crisp, if he were to roll up the heavens and be done with it, where would we be? What could we say?

Earlier generations knew this, but ours is the first that has had the capacity for universal self-destruction. One of the effects of the recent concern with global warming has been the growing interest in climate change, which threatens our entire planet. Already for many years now the Sahara Desert has been expanding at an alarming rate, and nomadic tribesmen right across Africa have been displaced from their homes. Long-standing drought in Australia has had much the same effect across broad swathes of the outback and no-one knows whether the areas that have dried up will ever be habitable again. At the other end of the spectrum, rising sea levels threaten a number of Pacific islands, which are likely to be submerged by around 2045 if present trends continue; and developed countries like the United Kingdom and the Netherlands wonder how much of their territory will be lost to the invading sea. There is even talk that the Gulf Stream will lose its force and cease to bring the warmth of the tropics to Western Europe, which may result in a catastrophic depopulation of much of the continent. In July 2002, the *National Geographic* magazine outlined what would happen to New Orleans if the wrong combination of flooding and hurricanes should occur. Little did the authors know that their report would be a blueprint for what actually happened just over three years later. Never before in history has there been such widespread awareness of the fragility of the ecosystem in which we live, and Christians have more cause than ever to remind the world that human beings are not the masters of their destiny, which so many of us think we are. The apocalyptic visions of the Bible have never seemed more real than at the present time, and there is solid scientific evidence to back them up.

There is not much we as individuals can do about such momentous things as climate change and global warming, which are likely to continue however much we may try to slow them down or even reverse them. Even so, we can and must adopt a more realistic approach to our own lives, economizing on fuel emissions where we can, recycling waste as far as possible and generally limiting our consumption to sustainable levels. At the same time, we have a duty to maintain the health and well-being of ourselves and our communities, and cannot allow the demand for economy to push us into organized deprivation, which would have even more harmful effects in the longer term. The nature of life is such that we have to live it every day; we cannot simply take a few weeks off and refuse to eat or sleep, without incurring some serious negative consequences. Some people have done things of that kind for various reasons, and there is a long tradition of Christian asceticism that advocates such practices, but even the most dedicated hermits cannot neglect themselves completely, and sooner or later must turn their thoughts towards the mundane business of survival. For most of us, however, heroic feats of self-denial are out of the question. Earth-bound as we are, we want to know where the next meal will be coming from, who is going to provide it and how much it will cost. Jesus understood this, of course, and the same Sermon on the Mount that contains the Lord's Prayer goes on to record the words with which he rebuked his disciples for their anxieties in this respect. Look at the birds of the air, he said, or the lilies of the field. They do not worry about such things, and God takes care of them. Do you not think he will take care of you too, since you are so much more valuable to him than they are (Matt. 6:26)? The words are familiar, but we must be honest and admit that most of the time their message passes us by. It is not that we disagree with our Lord, of course, but we feel that we just have to be practical about this kind of thing. Contemplating lilies is not going to put food on the table this evening, and for most of us there is really no option – nice as they are, the lilies will have to wait for another time.

It is astonishing how much there is in the Scriptures which strikes us in that kind of way. Perhaps you are one of those people who goes through your Bible highlighting verses that mean something special to you. If you are, you might like to try highlighting verses against which you might as well write NPA – no practical application. Doing this will require a high level of honesty, but if you do not cheat, you will be amazed at how many verses will rapidly acquire this marginal note. I would even be bold enough to suggest that a high proportion of them will occur in the sayings of Jesus himself, some of which are particularly hard to put into practice – 'sell what you possess and give to the poor' (Matt. 19:21), 'take up [your] cross and follow me' (Matt. 16:24), 'go, and from now on sin no more' (John 8:11). What kind of world was that man living in? Does he really expect me to do these things? It is a commonplace of popular, non-churchgoing Christianity that Jesus was a great teacher who offered a lot of excellent moral advice by which we should live our lives, but a closer reading of the New Testament will quickly demonstrate just how inadequate such a picture is. The more devout Jews of his day had devised a moral code they were comfortable with and followed more or less adequately. They were not bad people and were generally respected for their high standards of behaviour. Some of them, like the so-called 'rich young ruler', felt attracted to Jesus and his teaching because it seemed to tie in well with what they themselves already believed and practised (Matt. 19:16–22). Had he wished to, Jesus could probably have started a subset of Judaism by gathering such people together as his followers. He would have been greatly admired instead of suffering persecution, and, who knows – he might even have founded a megasynagogue in the suburbs of Jerusalem.

But Jesus did not do that. When high-minded and well-meaning people approached him, he did not welcome them on board and encourage them in their good works. Instead, he challenged them to consider what their real motives were. How much were they prepared to sacrifice in trying to do the will of God? Were they prepared to suffer hardship, endure pain and even submit to death because of their love for the Lord, or had they transformed the unsettling commands of God into badges of social and cultural superiority that salved their consciences, but left them further away from the kingdom of heaven than ever?

Looking back after more than two thousand years we know the answers to these questions, and it is tempting for us to conclude that because we know this, we actually do it in practice. Yet a quick look at the church in most developed countries will soon show that we are more like the rich young ruler than we care to think. Allowing for numerous individual exceptions, our churches are mostly made up of solid, middle-class types who want a safe and secure environment for themselves and their families. For them, the change that conversion brings to an individual is most evident in the lives of those whose previous behaviour was antisocial or harmful in some way, and who have now returned to the 'straight and narrow pathway', as they think of it, which corresponds remarkably well with the suburban lifestyle they have been living all along. To be fair, the notion that conversion might lead to the exact opposite, to someone leaving a comfortable way of life in order to camp out in some remote jungle or in the slums of a great city, is not unknown to them. But it is rather like the career of an acrobat – something to be admired from afar as the calling of a gifted minority, rather than something to be imitated in their own lives as the normal behaviour of a Christian.

The complacency of the majority in this respect can be particularly dangerous when it leads to movements of reaction against it. These occur periodically, when people revisit the words of Jesus and take them literally. In the early days of the church there were men who went into the desert to do battle with the devil, abandoning everything they had and living off whatever God might provide for them. These were the 'hermits' or 'monks', whose dedication gave them immense spiritual authority over the church, even if it never attracted more than a small minority of professed believers. As time went on, it came to be thought that if someone wanted to be a serious Christian, he or she should enter a religious community of that kind and abandon the 'world' to its own devices. That is what Martin Luther did as a young man, only to discover that he could not find peace with God in that way. In the end, Luther broke with the monastic tradition but encouraged his followers to apply its spiritual principles as best they could in their everyday lives. Anyone who now has a regular pattern of daily prayer and Bible reading has adopted what was once a monastic preserve, and the fact that we continue to encourage such habits shows just how valuable we have found them to be over the years.

In the Middle Ages, though, men like Francis of Assisi found the monasteries increasingly corrupt and removed from their primitive ideals, and so they tried to bring back the life of 'poverty, chastity and obedience' by once again renouncing everything and living as beggars off the charity of others. They became the 'friars', who started off by unsettling the comfortable piety of the

established church but ended up conforming to it in more ways
than one, particularly once the gifts of their devoted followers
began to make them rich. On the eve of the Reformation they
were going through a crisis of identity, and it is perhaps not surprising to find that many of them ended up in the camp of the
Reformers, having discovered that it was practically impossible for
them to implement their own high ideals.

Protestants tried to resolve this problem by reinterpreting the
demands of the Christian life. Instead of abandoning everything
and retreating into a monastic form of existence, believers were
told to take charge of their lives and possessions. Rich people were
not expected to throw everything away but to invest their wealth in
useful and productive ways, to benefit the whole of society. Trade
and industry were to be encouraged to provide widespread
employment and increase the national wealth, so that more people
could enjoy a higher standard of living. Nowadays we are used to
hearing horror stories about the exploitation of labour, and particularly of child labour, during the Industrial Revolution, but
although things were far from perfect at that time, the fact remains
that in the longer term, wealth was produced and more people
were able to enjoy its benefits. The affluent societies in which we
live today are the direct result of this. They have brought us to the
point where we have come to believe that 'our daily bread' is not
just an aspiration to be prayed for, but a natural right to be enjoyed
by everyone. This is a great blessing in many ways, but it has come
at a price. The sense of entitlement to a decent lifestyle, which so
many people in developed countries now take for granted,
whether they have worked for it or not, has not brought anyone
closer to God. People who have been relieved of the need to work
twelve hours a day for starvation wages have not devoted their
leisure time to the pursuit of spiritual things; indeed, a case could
easily be made for saying that the insatiable thirst for leisure activities is one of the great curses of our time and the source of so
much of the widespread decline in moral standards we observe
around us. Prosperity has dulled the spirit within us, and we get the
uncomfortable feeling that the biblical characters we resemble
most are those whom the prophets of Israel denounced for living
in luxury and ignoring the things of God. The prophets warned

that a terrible judgment awaited such people, and we may be sure that if it is really true that we resemble them, an equally terrible judgment awaits us also.

The sentence of the Lord's Prayer we are looking at now is the shortest in the entire text, but it is also the most pivotal. It stands at the intersection of heaven and earth, of the spiritual and the physical worlds in which we live. At one level it is so earthy and practical as to seem out of place when we put it alongside things like praying for the will of God to be done on earth or asking for the forgiveness of sins. Yet at another level it touches on the most fundamental question anyone can ask about our faith – does it actually work in practice? Is there a God out there who will provide for my daily needs or is it all an illusion, a nice idea that has no practical application to everyday life? There are thousands of people, perhaps millions, who think precisely that. For them, Christianity is a nice idea, but it just does not work. To live like Jesus may be possible for a few monks and eccentrics, but as a recipe for the average person, it is simply out of the question. Sadly, Christians themselves often provide the best evidence of this. Surveys have shown that churchgoing people live in almost exactly the same way as everyone else and that their faith makes practically no difference to their lives. Admittedly, this may be an exaggeration, since Christians are likely to fill their leisure time with church activities in a way other people do not, but as long as religion is regarded as no more than a hobby or a private interest, this will not affect the statistics. Studying the Bible is not the same thing as acting on it, so what difference does church attendance and involvement make? We need to ask ourselves this question, because while Christians are not called to be freaks or eccentrics, we are called to be different from the world in ways that touch the very foundations of our being.

If we are born again into a new life, then we must automatically be different from those who are not, and surely this difference ought to be noticeable. But how? Is it something meant to attract others or repel them? The truth of course is that it will attract some people and repel others, or, more precisely, it will attract most people in some ways and repel them in others. But how can we know which is which and whether we are really doing the right thing at any given moment? In asking God to supply our daily bread, we are not trying to buy into a kind of heavenly insurance policy. Still less are we forming ourselves into some sort of corporate elite that will be cushioned against the trials of daily life in a way that others are not. When we pray to God in this way, we are recognizing that everything we have is ultimately a gift from him and that it remains at his disposal. If what we have is his, then what we are must be his also. The more we are fed by him, the more we shall be dependent on him and the closer we shall be drawn to him. At its heart, this petition is a prayer for a deeper relationship with God, for a greater resemblance to him, for a life ultimately nourished from the same source as his own life – in short, for a transformation in which the image and likeness of God in us will become ever more faithful to the original from which that image was made, and as that happens, our life will become daily more closely entwined with his.

Give us

Our Lord Jesus Christ tells us to go to our Father and to speak directly to him: 'Give us'. The words may be those of a child who has not yet learned the social graces; they may be the words of a parent or social superior who feels free to address children or inferiors in this way; they may even be a cry for help. As I have already suggested, surely the last of these is the closest analogy here. Our relationship with God is one of great intimacy, but at the same time it is also one of total dependence on him. In some ways it is like the relationship of a child to his parents. Jesus uses that analogy to describe those who belong to the kingdom of heaven, but our walk with Christ only begins there (Matt. 19:14). Once we have been born again into God's eternal life, we are called to grow to maturity, because it is as fully formed spiritual adults, and not as immature babes, that he wants us to have fellowship with him in his kingdom (1 Cor. 13:11; Heb. 5:12–13).

There is no one human relationship that fully captures the relationship we have with God in Christ. We depend on him as inferiors, yet speak with him as equals, because he has invited us to do so. We are told to ask freely and boldly for what we need, because as our Father, God wants to give good gifts to his children. Yet at the same time, we cannot presume on his goodness or claim his gifts as a right (Matt. 7:7–11). Jesus calls us his friends, but at the same time makes it clear that this friendship is measured by our obedience to his commands (John 15:14).

It is important to remind ourselves of this because all too often our relationship with God is portrayed as a casual friendship, in which the Sovereign Lord of creation supposedly allows us to take liberties because of the intimate connection we have with him in Jesus Christ. As with so many portraits of this kind, there is some truth in it, but it also contains a serious distortion. It is true that God allows us into his presence and treats us as members of his family, but he remains our Father. The house we dwell in is his, and we never cease to be dependent on him for everything we have. This is right and proper, but inevitably it conditions the kind of friendship we have with him. If I am dependent on another person for my livelihood, I cannot regard him as an equal in the usual sense of the word, even if that is formally the case. For example, my boss at work may be a very nice person; outside the workplace we are equals, but he is still the boss and this will affect the way I view him, whether I am at work or not. We cannot really be 'friends' in the full sense of the word, just as teachers cannot be friends with their students for the same reason. In the normal run of things, friendship is a voluntary association of equals, and if that is how we understand it, we are not friends with God and never can be. We depend on him far too much for that.

This may sound harsh, but the other side of the coin is that friendships of that kind can be fragile, particularly if they come to involve obligations. I am very happy to have friends, but if they start asking me to do things for them, I become a bit wary. What sort of friendship do they have in mind? Are they interested in me for who I am or only for what I might be able to do for them? Are they socializing or networking? It is easy to be friendly when there is no cost involved, but this kind of friendliness vanishes as soon as there is a price tag attached to it. People you can rely on to support you when you need it, to help you out when you are down on your luck and to tell you the truth when you do not want to hear it – these people are rare, but they are the ones who are our true friends. Very often we cannot identify them until something

goes wrong in our lives and we discover that they are there, willing
to lend a hand. So true is this that we often take comfort by
reminding ourselves that only in such situations do we discover
who our real friends are!

If this is the way we understand friendship, then of course God
is our friend – the best one we can ever have. Furthermore, it is
not in unexpected circumstances after many years that we find this
out, but right at the beginning. Indeed, it is the very basis of our
relationship. The Lord's Prayer does not expressly say so, but Jesus
makes it clear elsewhere in the Sermon on the Mount that God is
ready and willing to give us what we ask, provided of course that it
is something we ought to have (Mark 7:7–8)! We know that he is
willing to do this because in fact he has already done it. We did not
ask him to send his Son from heaven to be our Saviour – the Son
came because he had agreed to do the Father's will, not because
anyone on earth had put in a request to that effect (Phil. 2:5–7).
This is so obvious that it is almost embarrassing to have to remind
ourselves of it, yet we rarely think through the implications it has
for our lives.

The ancient Israelites believed that God would eventually
redeem his people, and there were holy men and women among
them who waited patiently for the day when he would fulfil his
promise. We meet two of them, Simeon and Anna, when we read
about Mary and Joseph taking the baby Jesus to the temple to be
circumcised (Luke 2:25–38). But even they did not really know
how God's redemption would come about. Luke makes a point of
telling us that it was only by a special revelation from the Holy
Spirit that Simeon was able to confess that Jesus was the promised
Messiah, and, even then, it does not appear he was told that Jesus
was the Son of God.

Similarly, God sends his Holy Spirit into our hearts when we ask
for him (Luke 11:13; Acts 8:14–17). Jesus promised his disciples
that the Spirit would come, but they had no idea who the Spirit
was and did not really want him – at least not if his coming was
dependent on the prior departure of Jesus (cf. John 16:6). The disciples would have preferred it if Jesus had stayed with them, and
he had to make it clear to them that it would be to their advantage
for him to go away and send the Holy Spirit to take his place. The

Spirit brings God's gifts to his people, but distributes them according to his will and not ours (1 Cor. 12:11). I may be able to ask God to give me some particular gift, but in the end I must be content with the one(s) he has given me and not complain if I have not received what has been given to someone else. What he has chosen to give I can only receive with gratitude; I cannot send it back and exchange it for something I would rather have instead! God has promised to give each of his children what they need when they need it; to walk in faith is to believe we have been and will always be equipped with the blessings we need to see us on our way. There is no reason to doubt that these blessings will increase and grow as we go on to spiritual maturity, but the timing and the measure of the gifts lies in his sovereign power to give and is quite unrelated to what we might like to have at any particular moment.

The point I am making here is that when we ask the Father for our daily bread, we are not breaking new ground but merely asking someone who already has an established track record of giving, and whose gifts have already exceeded anything we could ask or think of, to fulfill his promises and extend his blessings to us also. Of course, we also have to remember the great gulf that separates the creature from the Creator. What we as creatures need from him is vitally important to us, but it is only a small thing for him. Jesus makes this point himself in the verses immediately following the Lord's Prayer, when he talks about the lilies of the field and so on (Matt. 6:25–34). This smallness, it should be understood, is not because we are unimportant to God. On the contrary, we are so important to him that he even sent his Son to save us. It is a small thing to God only in the sense that his riches are so inexhaustible that our needs barely make a dent in them. Here God truly stands head and shoulders above any human or earthly power. Our parents may be well-off but their resources are not boundless, and there comes a point in most of our lives when we are firmly told that we have had all there is to spare and can expect no more. When we get to adulthood we are expected to fend for ourselves, and children who remain dependent on their parents have not really grown up properly. Even the state cannot pay out for ever. There was a time not so long ago when many people thought it could, and would, and they came to rely on welfare benefits for their daily bread. But pressure on the system has increased, the number of beneficiaries has multiplied while the pool of contributors has remained static or even diminished, and demand is increasingly outstripping supply. One way or another, the welfare state is going out of business, forcing many people to look for alternative sources of future income, because its abundant resources have turned out not to be infinite after all.

When it comes to God, though, we never have to worry that we are asking him for more than he is able to give. Growing to spiritual maturity does not mean we are thrown out of the house and expected to earn a living for ourselves, but the very opposite. The more mature we are in Christ, the more we benefit from his gifts, because to be spiritually mature means to be ever more closely united to him. Nor do we have to worry that there will ever be too many claimants on his goodness for us to be able to get an adequate share of his benefits. Nothing could be more foolish than to suppose that if someone else becomes a Christian and starts asking God for things, there will be less available for us! In a paradoxical way, the conversion of others to Christ adds to my share of his blessings, because each newborn Christian is a blessing from God. Far from competing with each other for his favours, we are given gifts primarily for the purpose of sharing them with our brothers and sisters in Christ, so that together we may all grow to maturity in him (1 Cor. 12:12–26). It is as if each gift multiplies itself every time it is exercised, so that what is given to one turns out to be a blessing shared with all.

This is one reason why it is important to notice that we are taught to pray in the plural – 'give us'. The Lord's Prayer is not the petition of a private individual but the common supplication of the church, and the significance of this is nowhere more apparent than in this sentence of it. Nothing is more natural for children than to ask their parents for things for themselves. Only rarely would a child think to ask for something on behalf of someone else, and in this respect I am afraid that most of us are all too typical of children. We know what our own needs are and it is only natural that we should be preoccupied with them – but how much thought do we give for others? How aware are we of their needs in addition to our own? This is especially important in relation to the spiritual gifts discussed at such great length in 1 Corinthians 12 and 14. The whole point of the apostle Paul's remarks about them is that although they were given to individuals in the first instance, they were intended mainly for the edification of the church as a whole and not for the private enjoyment of the person concerned. This is obvious in the case of gifts like prophecy, teaching and evangelism, where the whole point of the gift is to communicate with others, but it is less apparent when it comes to something like speaking in tongues. As we discover when we read Paul's remarks on the subject, the tendency even for Christians to ignore the good of the whole in favour of the blessing of the individual was just as common in ancient Corinth as it is now. What is so interesting about this is not that Paul had to write to the church to tell them to regulate the exercise of their spiritual gifts so that the principle of general edification would not be forgotten, but that he assumed that the church had the power to do this. How can a human authority control the outpouring of God's Spirit? The answer Paul gives to this apparently contradictory statement is that 'the spirits of prophets are subject to prophets' (1 Cor. 14:32). What this means is that spiritual gifts are not to be confused with some form of spirit possession, in which the person possessed has no control over what he says or does. Such possession is certainly possible, but it is demonic, and the demon must be cast out of the person so afflicted (Acts 16:16–18).

To be filled with the Holy Spirit is altogether different from this, because the Spirit-filled person is a child of God and therefore has control of his gift just as the Son of God had control of his Spirit. This is an awesome privilege, testimony to the fact that God not only loves us as his children but trusts us as well. It is perfectly possible for a parent to demonstrate love for a child by giving him or her something to play with, but good parents will take the necessary precaution of making sure the toy is something that will not be able to do much harm to a child if it is mishandled. But God offers us the gift of his life-giving Spirit (Acts 2:38; Rom. 8:9–11). He will pour into us one who is able to burn and destroy, to heal and to build up. The Holy Spirit of God is not to be trifled with, because as Jesus reminds us, there is no forgiveness for those who fail to treat him with the proper respect (Matt. 12:31). The indwelling presence of the Holy Spirit in our hearts is an awesome privilege offered to Christians, and we must never forget the extent and depth of God's goodness to us in this way.

This is of particular relevance when it comes to the gifts of preaching and teaching, which are closely related to one another but not strictly the same. It is all too easy for a preacher to use the authority of his office for ends far removed from the kingdom of God. He may get carried away by the force of his own rhetoric, and start to believe he can persuade people of anything once he has them in his grip. He may be right about that, but if he is, he must be warned that he is in grave danger of blaspheming against the Holy Spirit by abusing his gift. Similarly, a teacher may easily communicate things that are false to those who lack the knowledge needed to discern right from wrong. If this is done in ignorance, it can be forgiven, but a teacher who decides to promote his own fantasies and prejudices as if they are the truth is in equal danger of quenching the power of the Spirit in the lives of those to whom he is called to minister. And if he does that, he will quench the Spirit in his own life as well. Spiritual gifts can be properly used only by spiritual people, and which of us can claim to be adequate for that? Only by constant dependence on God can we even begin to do the work he has entrusted to us. In giving us his gifts, God is really giving us himself. He is drawing nearer to us and strengthening us in our relationship with him, so that when we exercise our gifts we can do so in the knowledge that they will be used for the purpose for which they were originally given.

Today we are so self-centred that the good of others scarcely enters our heads most of the time unless it is something dramatic and unusual, like giving to charity relief, for instance. More mundane, everyday concerns tend to go by the board, despite all the lip-service we pay to fellowship and community. Ironically, nowhere is this attitude more visible than in our approach to public worship, the moment we come together to pray the Lord's Prayer! My home church, for example, has a number of different services designed to appeal to different groups within the congregation – the young, the old, the traditionally minded and so on. However, it is noticeable that there is a considerable body of people who choose not to come to the services not specifically

geared for them. More than once, when this behaviour has been
queried, the response has been 'I don't go because there's nothing
in it for me!' How they can be so sure of that I do not know, but
the underlying attitude this response reveals is surely quite frightening. Since when do we go to church merely when the service is
designed to suit us? One of the great beauties of the Anglican
common prayer is that it was not composed to suit the tastes of
particular individuals, and for centuries no-one thought that it
should have been. It is only very recently that this attitude has
come to the fore and that the church has fallen victim – there is no
other term for it – to the whims of the consumer generation.

The effects of this 'give me what I want' mentality are not hard
to find. In some cases, the whole concept of worship and ministry
has been altered to conform to its dictates. If a worship service
does not include the kind of music I happen to prefer, I shall not
go to it, with the result that many congregations gather on the sole
principle that the members all like the same kind of music. One of
my friends is a highly skilled organist who has the great privilege of
being able to play an organ he designed and had built himself. It is
a wonderful instrument, capable of playing the most sophisticated
organ concertos to acoustic perfection, but as my friend is only
too quick to point out, the congregation of the church where the
organ is does not want that. What they like are good old Moody
and Sankey hymns from the nineteenth century, most of which
were intended to be simple enough to be played by untrained
people on whatever instrument might be available. There is
nothing wrong with that of course, but the organist is frustrated
because he cannot persuade people to let him show them what the
instrument is capable of, in the hope that they might grow to like
it. By sticking with their established preferences they are unable to
grow and develop their tastes to accommodate anything else, and
in effect are missing out on the gift of both the organ and the
organist to the church.

At another level, there are those who say that if the church is not
prepared to ordain women or practising homosexuals, it is not
responding to their needs, and so it cannot be a faithful witness to
the gospel. This kind of argument would be dismissed as fatuous,
were it not for the fact that it has persuaded many leaders in the

mainline Protestant churches to bend their rules and traditions to accommodate something completely foreign to the teaching of Scripture. Similarly, there are those who say that if the church tries to insist on doctrines like the Trinity or the atoning work of Christ, it is not respecting their freedom to believe in the God of their own choosing. If they do not want a God who sends people to hell, then so be it – there can be no hell! So influential has this way of thinking become that many churches skate over such doctrines because they know that to emphasize them will only cause offence to members of their congregations. Once again, the idea that the preacher ought to be challenging the prejudices of his people and trying to get them to consider truths they do not naturally like or agree with seems to have been lost by the wayside. There are always parts of the Christian message that are hard for us to accept or understand. The right response to this is not to reject them or leave them to one side as if they are of no more than secondary importance, but to treat them as a challenge that has to be faced and overcome. I have often found that the most satisfying sermons I have preached are ones that have been expositions of the passages I find most difficult to understand, because they have forced me to wrestle with the biblical text until I could make sense of it and submit my mind and my heart to its teaching – however uncongenial that may have been at the beginning.

The problem with pandering to the whims and fancies of particular individuals is that there will inevitably come a point where their eccentricities can no longer be adequately catered for without seeing the whole institution fall apart. This is at least part of what has been happening recently in the Anglican Communion as well as in other mainline Protestant churches around the world. Liberal clergy in America and elsewhere have promised certain minority groups that their aspirations will be fully met within the established church, and are shocked when they discover considerable opposition to this. Understandably, many of those who believe the promises are disillusioned and turn away from the church altogether, because, in their eyes, it has failed to keep its word to them. They are wrong to blame the church for this, of course, but right to claim that they have been misled by those who have reached out to them in this way. The truth is that the church cannot bend to accommodate everything and everyone without losing its identity and witness, and those who try to make it do so will always be disappointed in the end.

Pretending that this is not true gets us nowhere, and pressure groups that put their own selfish interests ahead of the good of the whole can only divide the body of Christ. The plural form 'give us' must be taken to mean what it says and not be privatized into something that applies only to me and to those who think the way I do. A gift that divides the church is no gift at all, but a trick of the devil, who has been having the time of his life lately in our churches. It is high time for Christians to remind ourselves of this important principle, which theologians have called 'catholicity'. What is given by God is given to all, and when something that claims to be a gift of God cannot be received by all because it contradicts fundamental Christian principles, it is time to ask where the gift really comes from and what its intended purpose really is.

This day

When Jesus tells us to ask God to give us what we need, he specifies that we should add that the gift is intended for 'this day' – the first reference to time in the prayer. At one level the meaning seems to be clear enough. We are told to pray to God for our immediate needs. This is not because the longer term does not matter, although we must bear in mind that Jesus did in fact tell his disciples to live one day at a time (Matt. 6:34). In one sense, it is like the old Chinese proverb, which says that a journey of a thousand miles begins with a single step. If we do not start where we are and deal with the immediate problems that confront us, we shall never be able to move on to higher things. If we try, we shall find that our earlier lack of preparation and foresight will keep holding us back. It is also a challenge to us to expect that God will come to our aid right here and now. One of the criticisms sometimes made of Christian evangelism is that it promises converts that they will have 'pie in the sky when they die' but does not do much to relieve their physical distress here and now. Such accusations are a gross distortion of the truth and have never been typical of Christian missionary efforts, but if anyone is tempted to think that way, the Lord's Prayer cuts them dead. To pray for our daily bread is not to ask for something that will only materialize in some distant, eschatological future, but for food that will appear on the table today and give us the strength we need for tomorrow.

We cannot escape the immediacy of the challenge. God has promised that he will take care of us and make a difference in our lives here and now. Many people can testify that soon after they became Christians they found themselves in some unexpected trouble that severely tested their faith. Perhaps they lost a job, or contracted an illness. Maybe they went through a painful bereavement or break-up of a relationship. Perhaps none of these things was directly connected to their conversion, and they might have happened anyway, but the timing was such as to put the reality of their new spiritual life on the line. Would the God whom they had so recently come to believe in help them get through something as awful as this?

We must admit that some people will say they prayed to God in circumstances like these, received no answer, and abandoned their faith as a result. However, it usually turns out that such people were never really believers at all. They were not in the habit of walking with God in a daily life of prayer and contemplation and only turned to him as a last resort. Having tried everything else and seen it fail, they were finally reduced to prayer! In their minds, God was something like a heavenly vending machine. You put your prayer in the slot, make your selection and wait for the right answer to come out. If it fails to materialize, you shake the machine in the hope of persuading it to disgorge its contents, and if that fails, you kick it in frustration, count your losses and move on to something else. This is not faith, and God does not want or need followers like that. We should therefore not be surprised that people who pray in this way are not normally heard.

It is a very different story with those who have been born again into a living faith. These people do not reduce God to a convenience who can be drawn on when needed and ignored the rest of the time. Those of us who know him personally and who walk with him on a daily basis know that he is taking care of us each step of the way. We do not have any privileged position in the world that guarantees us success, nor is our faith a heavenly insurance policy that protects us against any possible harm. In the secular world, we are just as susceptible as anyone else to economic misfortune, physical illness and death. We may be unable to scale the heights of success in sports, the media or our professional life, perhaps at least partly because our commitment to Christ makes us less determined than others to succeed and therefore less willing to sacrifice our lives in the effort needed to get to the top. Many Christians have walked away from lucrative career opportunities because they have preferred to serve the Lord in a humbler, but ultimately more rewarding capacity, and in earthly terms they have paid a price for this. There is certainly no guarantee that just because we are believers we shall have unlimited prosperity in this world, or form an exclusive social and economic elite. If all you want in life is to become rich, it is not a good idea to put your faith in Jesus, as he himself warned his disciples on more than one occasion (Matt. 19:24; Luke 16:19–25).

What Christians bear witness to is not success, as measured in worldly terms, but survival. This may not seem like much at first sight, but to those who have been battered by all that life can throw at them, survival is a very precious thing. Moreover, we are not talking here about survival in some vegetative state almost worse than death, but about a life of renewed hope and vigour. Very often it turns out that people who have been forced to leave a job or abandon a relationship that has kept them going have in fact been given a new lease of life, with new opportunities and new expectations. It is obviously not easy, after many decades of marriage, to face the prospect of widowhood and yet thousands of people must do this every year. It is almost built into the marriage contract that one of the partners will outlive the other, and in the majority of cases it is the woman who survives her husband. In traditional Hindu culture such a prospect was so unappealing that it led to the custom of *sati*, according to which a widow was burnt alive on her late husband's funeral pyre. To Christians, such a practice is an abomination because we know that God's grace and goodness towards us is such that he is able to bring new life even out of such a tragedy. In our minds, the greatest respect a surviving spouse can pay to his or her loved one is to go on living and working for God in the years that remain, whether that takes the form of remarriage or continuing, but productive, widowhood.

This is the teaching of the apostle Paul and its truth has been borne out time and again in the lives of those who have submitted themselves to it (1 Cor. 7:39–40; 1 Tim. 5:3–16).

What is true in the case of widowhood is true also in the many other afflictions we may be called to suffer in this life. The great nineteenth-century hymn writer Fanny Crosby was blinded by disease at the age of six months, but she lived to be ninety-five years old and became one of the great devotional writers of the church. When asked whether she regretted her blindness, she is said to have replied that she rejoiced in the knowledge that the first person she would see when her vision was restored would be the Lord Jesus, seated on his throne in heaven. Her much younger contemporary Helen Keller was even more severely afflicted, yet she gave her life to Christ, trusted in God for his goodness towards her in spite of all apparent evidence to the contrary, and is remembered today for the pioneer work she accomplished in helping others in her position to receive the assistance they needed. Few people have attained the fame of these great women, but their testimony has been echoed by millions. Whatever our circumstances may be, however we may have been afflicted in our lives, the loving hand of God is there to bring us through, to open a new door and to provide for our ongoing needs. We ask him for help today, and today is when we receive the comfort and assistance we need.

This brings us naturally to one of the most fundamental teachings of Jesus about our spiritual state before God. His message was that the time had come, that the day of salvation had arrived, and that a decision had to be made before it was too late. Dithering and delay were to be avoided at all costs, because once the moment had passed it would not come again. The parable of the rich fool still strikes a chill into the heart of everyone who reads it:

'I will tear down my barns and build larger ones, and there I will store all my grain and my goods. And I will say to my soul, Soul, you have ample goods laid up for many years; relax, eat, drink, be merry.' But God said to him, 'Fool! This night your soul is required of you, and the things you have prepared, whose will they be?' (Luke 12:18–20)

Those familiar with Morning Prayer in the Anglican tradition will know that it opens with a call to worship taken straight from Psalm 95: 'Today, if you hear his voice, harden not your hearts as in the day of temptation in the wilderness, when your fathers tempted me and saw my works . . .'[1] When God speaks, the time to respond is now, because the daily bread he wants to give us will not keep till tomorrow. This picture is not a fanciful one. Jesus compared the kingdom of heaven to a great banquet to which many different people had been invited. But when they heard about it, instead of dropping everything to attend, they began to make excuses. One had just bought a piece of property he needed to inspect, another had just acquired five yoke of oxen and a third was newly married. They were busy with other things and had no time to spare, so they were simply passed over and their places were taken by others who, on the face of it at least, had much less entitlement to be there (Luke 14:16–24).

The warning to us is clear. Sometimes we are given no choice at all, and God stops us in our tracks whether we like it or not. That is what happened to Saul of Tarsus on the road to Damascus, and it can still happen to people today (Acts 9:3–5). But most of the time his approach to us is less dramatic, more like the invitation to the banquet than like a thunderbolt from heaven. And what do we do then? Do we make excuses like those who were invited in the story Jesus told (Luke 14:16–24)? Do we think, as they thought, that there will be time to think about eternity later on? It is easy for young and active people, in particular, to imagine that they have all the time in the world to worry about such things and to put them off without thinking. But tragedy can hit us at any age and nobody can say when the thunderbolt from heaven will strike. We may escape for a time, but in the end it will come for us and we shall be unprepared. Jesus tells us that hell will be full of people who are wise from hindsight; do we want to be among them? From what we can tell, it seems that even they would prefer us to make up our minds while there is still time, but they are not allowed to come

---

1. Ps. 95:7–9, quoted in Heb. 3:7–9, where the spiritual application is made plain in what follows (vv. 12–19).

back and warn us of what awaits us if we do not (Luke 16:27–31). Now is the time, today is the day of salvation. The daily bread is on the table waiting for the banquet to begin. The only question is – where are we?

The importance of living in the present cannot be stressed too much. Many of us are inclined to look over our shoulders to what has happened in the past, either for good or for bad, and others worry unduly about what might happen at some point in the future. Either approach to life is a recipe either for doing nothing, or for doing the wrong thing. It is always good to be mindful of our heritage and to learn from history, but if this becomes a pre-occupation to the detriment of what we are called to do right now, it becomes a barrier to our relationship with God and with other people and not a help to it. We are all familiar with the kind of person who is forever digging up some past event and using it as an excuse for not moving forward in the present, and we know that this is often a recipe for inertia. But as Christians we have to remember that our past is behind us, that our sins are forgiven, that what we have done will not be held against us on the day of judgment.

If this is so with God, how much more ought it to be the case in our dealings with one another? Bearing grudges and letting them determine our conduct has no place in the Christian life, and we must be on our guard against this temptation. At the same time, worrying too much about the future can be equally dangerous. Some people will not do anything because they are afraid of what might happen, and there are times when this attitude becomes par-ticularly prevalent, as happened in the run-up to the coming of the present millennium. In 2005, a man who had stored up five years of provisions in the year 2000, just in case, finally decided to dispose of them, having concluded that the danger has passed – at least for the moment. That may be an extreme case, but lesser ver-sions of it can be found everywhere we look. How many plans have never been realized, how many projects have never got off the ground, merely because somebody has determined in advance that since there is no guarantee that they will ever be finished, there is no point starting? Fear of possible consequences can be taken to such extremes that doing nothing is seen to be the best course, and opportunities that should be seized and exploited are passed up. The history of Christian missions is full of such stories, not least in the inner cities and suburbs of the rapidly secularizing Western world. Our own lives may become a catalogue of failure simply because we have not had the courage to move forward when the door was open, and when we decided to do so it was too late. Now is the time, today is the day of salvation!

To live one day at a time is to plan ahead on the basis of current conditions and be prepared to modify them as and when that becomes necessary. Nobody should undertake something that does not allow for a certain flexibility, a plan B that can be implemented if the initial project fails to work out as expected. A classic example of failure to do this must surely be the German invasion of Russia in the summer of 1941. Adolf Hitler had determined that the country would be knocked out in a few months and so he made no provision for the Russian winter. But the invasion ran into unforeseen difficulties. It got bogged down, winter came and the army was caught in a trap for which it had not been prepared. We may be grateful for this, of course, but the lesson is one that must give us pause for thought. If we live one day at a time, we remain open to the possibility of sudden change, which may be imposed on us by events beyond our control. Are you ready for dealing with things that might happen without warning? Of course, you cannot predict everything that might occur, but it is the ability and willingness to adapt to circumstances that is required, not the gift of prophecy. It is never wise to be so locked into something that there is no possible escape, particularly if the something is a major drain on resources that cannot easily be met. 'Sufficient for the day is its own trouble' warned Jesus, a wise piece of advice we would do well to bear in mind as we look ahead (Matt. 6:34).

This day must be our immediate concern because it is where we are. Some people have an uncanny ability to ignore their present circumstances in the hope that something better will turn up if they just sit back and wait for it. This tendency was immortalized by Charles Dickens in the person of Mr Micawber (*David Copperfield*), who was always sitting around doing nothing for just that reason. In the end, he and his family went off to Australia to make a new life for themselves, but people like them would never be admitted there as immigrants nowadays. No country will willingly admit people who lack initiative, and the kingdom of heaven is little different in this respect. The wise man is warned in Scripture that now is the time, and that we have a responsibility to act in the present. This is important because it reminds us that God is always present in our lives. He was there in the past, yes. He will be there in the future, certainly. But he is there now, and now is the time to do something about it or else it will never get done.

Of course, as always in the Bible, there is another dimension to this that also has to be taken into consideration. We are accustomed to dividing time into a sequence of past, present and future. Strictly speaking, though, only the past and the future are genuinely temporal concepts. The present has no duration and is therefore not in time at all. The minute I say 'now' it is past and cannot be brought back again. In practice, the 'present' tends to mean the recent past and the immediate future but this is a pragmatic arrangement with no basis in fact. The present does not exist in time, but it is a concept we can hardly do without, since if we did not have it, we would not be able to distinguish the past from the future. The present is therefore necessary for us to be able to measure time, even though it is not part of it. It is important to grasp this because the Bible consistently uses the present to describe God, who dwells not in time but in eternity. Eternity is the permanent present, and our possession of this concept is a window into the mind of God. When we are told in Scripture that today is the day of salvation, we are being asked to understand that at the moment of our conversion, time and eternity intersect, and we whose days on earth are numbered are born again into eternal life. That life can never be taken away from us because it lies outside time; it does not have a 'before' or an 'after' and so once we have it, nothing can take it away from us. This is why we can never lose our salvation, because we have entered a dimension of reality where the time sequence that would be needed for such a loss to occur does not exist.

The problem we face is that we are still living in a time-conditioned universe and can only interpret eternity in relation to it. Things that are temporal can be used as analogies of things that are eternal because they share certain characteristics with each other, even though they function in completely different dimensions, but we must always remember that no analogy can provide a complete understanding of reality. The birth process is a prime example of this. Spiritual birth resembles physical birth to the extent that it is the beginning of a whole new existence, but the resemblance ends there. In spiritual birth, there is no gestation period, there are no labour pains and there is no afterbirth. It is not a process but an event that, even if it dawns on us over a period of time, nevertheless represents something eternally present in the mind of God. Because it is eternal, it is always present with him; it is only we who are in time who experience it as a new beginning. This is why the Bible says that we have been predestined for salvation. From God's perspective, that is simply another way of saying that we are eternally present as his children in his mind, regardless of what we perceive to be happening to us in time. When we become conscious of this we feel as if something new has begun in us, but in God we have been there all along and our fellowship with him will never change.

When we pray to God to reach out to us 'this day', our sense of being present in time reaches out to his presence in eternity and we connect with him in that way. A relationship between finite creatures like ourselves and our infinite Creator would not be possible otherwise. If we were totally time-bound, we would have no conception of the present and would therefore be incapable of relating in any way to eternity. But as it is, we live in a time-free present and it is the perspective from which we judge the passage of time around us. It is something of the divine image that God has placed in us and that makes us quite different from the other creatures here on earth. By rising above time and passing judgment on it we enter a new time-free dimension of reality, which is the dimension of Almighty God. There is no escape from this – *now* is the time, *today* is the day of salvation. If we ignore his summons to us, we shall perish, because we shall be cut off from his life that is eternal and alone is the source of the new creation we have become in Christ.

Our daily bread

We come now to the substance of the matter, our daily bread. At the most basic physical level, it is clear what this must mean. Bread stands for food and nourishment in general, and the word is frequently used in that way even today. By extension it may also mean the income that enables us to buy the food we need and from there it may even stretch to include the resources from which our income derives. If we dig into the history of the word, we shall discover that it has many social ramifications that escape everyday notice but that tell us a lot about the way we live. A 'companion', for example, is someone who shares our bread, and a 'company' is the association of those who eat together from a common source. The words were originally used in Roman military jargon, and their relevance to the Christian life can be seen from the way in which the New Testament frequently compares our spiritual experience to a soldier's career (Eph. 6:10–20; 2 Tim. 4:7). The fact that the breaking of bread stands at the centre of Christian fellowship only serves to intensify the link, even though it is clear that its origin lies elsewhere. The early church saw itself as God's army in a hostile world, a company of saints bound together by drawing its sustenance from a common source.

The mention of 'our daily bread' here recalls the experience of the people of Israel on their wilderness journey, and it is virtually certain that Jesus had this in mind when he included this sentence in his prayer. Deprived of food and faced with the possibility of starvation, the Israelites asked Moses to intercede for them with God. Moses did so and God replied by sending them manna, a breadlike substance that appeared early every morning in sufficient quantities to enable them to gather enough for the day ahead. They could not keep it overnight, however, and if they tried to do so, it went bad. The one exception to this was the day of preparation for the Sabbath, when the people were permitted to gather manna for two days and it did not rot overnight (Exod. 16:1–36). Manna was therefore 'daily bread' in the most literal sense of the term. It was a reminder to the people of Israel that their walk with God was not a once-a-week affair but something that had to be renewed daily if they were to survive at all. It went bad every twenty-four hours as a sign to them that they had to trust God one day at a time. So important was manna in the spiritual experience of Israel that centuries later it was still kept in the ark of the covenant at Jerusalem as a reminder of the days when the Israelites had depended on it for their daily sustenance (Exod. 16:33–34; Heb. 9:4).

God's provision would not fail his people, but for this promise to become a reality they had to have faith. It is easy to imagine how the Israelites might have thought that the coming of the manna was a one-off event, not to be repeated or relied on. We can sympathize with those who thought that they had to gather as much as they could while it was available, because in the desert there was no telling when or whether they would ever see it again. But Israel's journey through the wilderness was far more than just a voyage from one place to another. It was a time of spiritual testing in its own right, a generation-long exercise designed to root the evil of Egypt out of their system and prepare them for a new life in the Promised Land. For centuries, Christians of many different traditions have seen it as a prototype of the spiritual life, which they interpret as deliverance from sin (represented by the time of slavery in Egypt), the passage through the desert of this world for the span of a normal human lifetime, and finally the entry into the Promised Land of heaven. The modern mind hesitates to accept such typology, but in this case it seems to be a reasonable application of Israel's collective experience to our own individual ones. The years in the desert were indeed a time of testing and of preparation, and although the generation that escaped from Egypt was slated to die in the wilderness, their children would inherit the land that had been promised to their ancestors so long before. In our case, life on earth is also a time of testing and preparation, though when we die it will not be our children who will inherit the Promised Land but ourselves, when we shall be brought back to a new kind of life in another world.

The first thing to say about the daily bread, therefore, is that it is a call to faith. We would not ask God to provide something we do not believe exists, and the prayer for our daily bread is an expression of our belief that our basic needs will be provided as long as we need them. God has not put us on earth in order to starve us out at some stage: as long as the sun and moon endure there will be seedtime and harvest, summer and winter – the cycle of the seasons on which our livelihood ultimately depends (Gen. 8:22). But although we know from experience that this cycle is likely to continue, we cannot be certain about the details, and ultimately we walk in faith, even as we go forward into an apparently predictable future. The general pattern is clear enough, but there is no way of telling when or for how long it may be interrupted by droughts, plagues, hurricanes, fires and the other natural disasters we have to contend with, not to mention the man-made problems of over-farming and overpopulation. Within the broad picture sketched out in Genesis, there are swings from times of plenty, when food mountains pile up and we can hardly give it all away, to times when too many people are chasing too few resources. All we can really do about this is pray and hope for the best, remembering to lay aside provisions in the seven fat years for the leaner times that are almost sure to follow eventually (Gen. 41:25–36).

The second thing to notice about the daily bread is that Jesus had in mind a spiritual sustenance as well as a physical one. The manna that the people ate in the desert came from heaven and was a gift of God. It fed their bodies but also restored their spirits at a time when they were on the verge of despair. 'I am the bread which came down from heaven,' Jesus said, in a clear reference to the manna which, like the rock that followed the people in the desert and gave them the equally essential life-giving water, was a symbol of Christ (John 6:41). It was he who fed the people daily, and though they did not realize it at the time, he fed them with himself in the form of manna. Every time the people ate it they drew closer to God, because they understood that this was his special provision for their welfare, but it was only in the New Testament that what had really been going on was revealed.

In telling his disciples to pray for their daily bread, Jesus is telling us to pray for a deeper experience of him. The privations that could afflict the body were as nothing compared to the afflictions that beset the soul, and the wise man would soon learn that he did not live by bread alone, but by every word that pro-ceeds out of the mouth of God. The Word of God was none other than Jesus Christ, the Word made flesh, and it was on that heavenly manna that his people were summoned to feed – daily.

Here we must pause for a moment and reflect on how this command has been interpreted in the course of church history. In Roman Catholic devotional theology, it has become identified with the bread of Holy Communion, which in Catholic eyes is transubstantiated into the body of Christ. Transubstantiation is the belief that the consecrated bread and wine retain their outward form (their 'accidents') but are changed in their underlying, invisible 'substance'. To pray for daily bread has therefore often been interpreted by Roman Catholics to mean attending daily mass, which becomes the foundation of the spiritual life. Protestants have never gone to that extreme, and the rejection of transubstantiation as a doctrine was one of the most important aspects of the Reformation. Nowadays Roman Catholic theologians have great difficulty in defending their traditional teaching, if only because the substance–accidents distinction on which it is based is no longer tenable as a scientific theory of matter, but the renewal of liturgy since the 1960s has led to far more frequent celebrations of Holy Communion among Protestants, and this has been accompanied by a tendency to emphasize a more sacramental approach to God. As a result, just when it appears that a central teaching of the Protestant reformers has finally made its way into the heart of Roman Catholic thinking, the old, rejected doctrine seems to be making something of a comeback in Protestant circles that had supposedly rejected it!

Identification of the bread of the Eucharist with the body of Christ is not entirely false, although to extrapolate from that to the point where the Lord's Prayer becomes a justification for daily mass would seem to be taking things too far. Protestants would argue that although the daily spiritual bread for which we are told to ask is indeed the presence of Jesus Christ, that presence comes to us not in supposedly transubstantiated bread but in the Word of God we read in the Bible. It is on that Word that we are told to meditate day and night if we wish to draw nearer to God (Ps. 1:2). It is that Word which is the spiritual food that nourishes us from one day to the next. The eucharistic elements are an extension of the Word and bear witness to it but they cannot be understood or used properly apart from it. Frequent Communion is not a spiritual benefit if it is not accompanied by equally frequent teaching

of the Word, and in this respect it has to be said that the modern
church is in a spiritual crisis. The reality is that as eucharistic celebrations have multiplied, so preaching has declined, with the
result that Holy Communion has often become just another part
of worship with no real significance to those who partake of it in
the normal course of events. Incredible as it may seem, the
significance of the act has been taken to justify its frequent celebration, to the exclusion of all other considerations. Instead of
heightening its importance, familiarity has bred contempt and few
people now have any idea why the Lord's table stands at the
centre of our common life as Christians. Having starved ourselves of the Eucharist in the past, we are now eating it all the
time, and in the process it often seems we have lost our taste for
the food.

To gauge just how far we have strayed from traditional
Protestant practice, read the old exhortations in the 1662 Book of
Common Prayer, or study the preparations that used to precede
and mark out the Presbyterian Communion season. Coming to
the table to receive the bread and wine of the new creation was
not a routine event, but a moment of crisis and challenge for the
prospective communicants, who were told to examine their
hearts, to see whether they were worthy to partake of such a feast.
They were asked to consider their sins, to repent of them, to
make peace with their neighbours, to resolve to lead a new life and
then – and only then – to come to the table itself. It is true of
course that there were many who communicated infrequently
because they did not see themselves as being worthy enough to do
so, but although this was a misunderstanding, it was surely prefer-
able to the attitude that pays no special attention to it at all. There
is at least one well-known incidence of someone who was actually
converted through this time of preparation for the sacrament,
and we do well to remember his experience. He was the great
Cambridge preacher and evangelist Charles Simeon. Simeon came
to faith in Christ when he was preparing himself for Communion,
because he realized that he could not in good conscience receive
the bread in his current state of mind. But rather than stay away
from the table on the ground that he was unworthy, Simeon got
down on his knees, repented of his sinful ways and gave his life to

Christ. In theological terms, he made himself worthy in the only way he could, by dying to sin and rising again to a new life in Jesus.

The symbolism of Holy Communion demonstrates to us what this means and how it can come about in our lives as well. Christ is the bread who came down from heaven as the manna of old did, but he is also the bread that was broken for us. 'Breaking of bread' was an expression commonly used for a meal, particularly one at which guests were present. The expression occurs fairly often in ancient literature and does not necessarily have a special theological significance, but in the Eucharist it most certainly does have one. It was on the night that he was betrayed that Jesus took bread, and when he had blessed it, he broke it, saying, 'This is my body which is for you. Do this in remembrance of me' (1 Cor. 11:24). The transformation of the significance of this act from one plane of reality to another is clearly indicated in Scripture, immediately after the resurrection of Jesus. Following the harrowing events of the Friday on which he was crucified, his dejected followers dispersed in different directions. The disciples themselves stayed together in Jerusalem, but others less closely associated with Jesus made their way back to their homes in different parts of the country.

One of these was Cleopas, who went with a friend of his back to his home in Emmaus.[2] On the road, they were overtaken by a stranger who engaged them in conversation about the events of the previous few days, in the course of which he was able to expound to them the spiritual meaning of Jesus' death, as that had been foretold in the Old Testament. Given that Cleopas and his companion were not among the inner circle of the disciples, it is perhaps not surprising that all this struck them as fundamentally new, since they would not have heard the teaching Jesus had given to the twelve on their own. When they got to Emmaus, the companions asked the stranger in for the night, and in traditional Middle Eastern fashion, they sat down to a meal together. Luke

---

2. A village that lay about a day's journey to the west of Jerusalem. Whether it was on the same site as the modern Imwas is a matter of dispute.

describes what happened next in words that still move us today when we read them:

> When he was at table with them, he took the bread and blessed and broke it and gave it to them. And their eyes were opened, and they recognized him. And he vanished from their sight. They said to each other, 'Did not our hearts burn within us while he talked to us on the road, while he opened to us the Scriptures?' (Luke 24:30–32)[3]

What had started as a homely meal together had been transformed into an event of cosmic significance, which recalled and re-presented nothing less than the sacrifice and death of Jesus Christ on the cross. From that moment, the breaking of bread among Christians would have a special spiritual significance, understood (in the light of the incident at Emmaus) as a warming of the heart caused by the teaching of the inner meaning of the Scriptures that believers bring to conscious expression in their common fellowship meal.

Why did the bread have to be broken? Was it not enough for the heavenly manna to come down, to teach us about its place of origin and to connect us to it? Why did Jesus have to die? The first and fundamental reason for this is that death was the price demanded for human sin (Ezek. 18:4). This may seem extreme to some people, but the logic of it is clear. God is life and the only source of life for his creatures. To rebel against him, to disobey his commandments, is to reject that life, and the rejection of life is death. By taking our sins upon himself, Jesus condemned himself to death, since that was the only way our sins could be paid for and their deadly effects be removed from our lives. This act of expiation had to be performed by the sinless Son of God, because no sinful human being was capable of bringing us a life he did not himself possess. Even the high priest had to make sacrifices for his own sins, and could not presume to forgive the sins of other people (Heb. 5:3). It was only because Jesus had no sin that he could take our sins upon himself and pay the price God's justice

---

3. The entire episode is recounted in vv. 13–35.

demanded for them. The second reason why Jesus died is that without passing through death there can be no new life. The sinful, corrupt life we live here on earth has to be replaced with a pure life that can come only from heaven, and what is replaced is called 'death'. It is a removal of the old to permit the installation of the new.

Not long before the people of Israel cried out for manna in the desert, bread had played another role in their lives, and the significance of this now comes into play. Before leaving Egypt, the Israelites had participated in a communal meal that was to become one of the most solemn festivals in the Jewish year – the feast of the Passover. For this they had made bread, but because of their haste to depart they did not wait to leaven it. Unleavened bread (food they continued to use at Passover) thus became the symbol of their religious purity, and it rapidly became a hallmark of their faith. In later times, they would speak of leaven as if it were a kind of corruption; this usage is familiar to us from the New Testament. When Christians were summoned to celebrate the feast of Christ's resurrection, the new Passover, it was 'not with the old leaven, the leaven of malice and evil, but with the unleavened bread of sincerity and truth' (1 Cor. 5:8). The spiritual significance of bread could not have been clearer, and Jesus understood perfectly well what he was doing when he made it a central part of his teaching ministry. There is however an important difference, which makes the Christian feast something more than the Jewish Passover. In the Passover meal, the unleavened bread represents only one aspect of the people's deliverance. Of greater spiritual significance is the sacrifice of the lamb, which was eaten to symbolize the nation's participation in the sacrifice the high priest made for their sins on the day of Atonement. What were celebrated by Jews as separate events were brought together by Jesus at the Last Supper in the single act of eating the bread. The traditional meaning of the broken bread took on the additional significance of the lamb who was slain from before the foundation of the world; the body of Christ the high priest and the atoning sacrifice he made were fused into one. Here the symbolism of the broken bread is particularly powerful, because it is only when the bread is broken that it is eaten, and only when it is broken that it can serve its purpose of giving new life to those who partake of it. In his death is our life – here indeed is the heart of the mystery of our salvation.

When I break bread and take it into my body, I am reaffirming my commitment not only to the bread that came down from heaven in the man Jesus Christ but also, and more significantly, to the bread broken for me on the cross of Calvary. In the Eucharist I am partaking of the atoning work he did on my behalf. Of course the rite is a symbolic one, but it is no less important for that. For a start, it emphasizes the close connection there is between spiritual and physical life. By taking the consecrated bread into my physical body, I bear witness to the fact that I have been born again in every way and to every degree. It is not just the part of me that is conscious and intelligent which experiences this, but every aspect of my being. In the general resurrection at the end of time, I shall not be some kind of disembodied spirit floating through the ether. Rather, my body will be transformed and integrated into the heavenly dimension just as Jesus' body was, although I do not yet know precisely what that will be like (1 Cor. 15:35–58).

Furthermore, the Lord's Supper is a shared meal. I am not the only one to have been saved, nor is the gospel specially reserved for me. It is a shared inheritance, and all who are born again in Christ partake of it together. This is one reason why most Protestant churches insist that the congregation must consist of at least three people before a eucharistic celebration can take place. Anything less than that would compromise this essential communal aspect, which is why the Roman Catholic practice of the 'private mass', in which the priest is the sole participant, has consistently been rejected by the Reformed churches. The lower limit of three might be objected to on the ground that Jesus said 'where two or three are gathered in my name, there am I among them' (Matt. 18:20), but although that is true, it does not justify having Communion when only two people – the celebrant and a single communicant – are present. To mention but one possible difficulty, the two concerned might be married to each other and therefore in the eyes of God be one flesh. Having three present avoids this possibility; there will always be one who does not fit, as it were, and who can provide the symbolic link to the wider fellow-ship of the church, which the Eucharist exists to proclaim.

Next, the broken bread is the symbol of the heavenly banquet at which Christ will preside for ever. It will be an everlasting bridal feast and the church, which includes you and me, will be the bride (Rev. 21:2; Luke 22:30). The eucharistic meal is the foretaste of that heavenly feast at which the Bread of heaven broken for us will preside and distribute his blessings to the redeemed for all eternity. Then 'give us this day our daily bread' will be realized in all its eternal fullness, as the Christ who gave himself for us once for all on the cross will give himself to us in the light of the day that will have no end. In the Eucharist, the broken bread is shared equally with all the communicants, because we all belong to the one body (1 Cor. 10:16–17). Christ died for all, his body was broken for all, and we are all members of his broken, risen and glorified body in heaven. It is in and through that broken body that we are presented to the Father as worthy to stand in his presence, because the broken body has done for us what we cannot do for ourselves – brought us forgiveness of sin by making full atonement for it. In the broken body our sins are not wiped away as if they never had any real existence and can simply be airbrushed out of the picture completely. Rather, the wounds of the broken, but now risen, ascended and glorified body of Christ remain to remind us that those sins have been paid for in full, and that the price of our redemption remains present and active in the heart of God.

Finally, the broken bread of the Eucharist challenges us by reminding us that we need the heavenly manna in order to go on with our journey into God. When we take that bread and drink the cup that represents the blood he shed for us, we commit ourselves afresh to the spiritual struggle that is transforming our lives in preparation for the eternal banquet of heaven. I do not myself cel-ebrate the Eucharist very often, but when I do, I always try to encourage people to think of the occasion as an opportunity to take the next step in their journey with God. This may mean repentance for some unconfessed sin, it may mean a renewed determination to take up our cross and follow him, it may mean a renewed commitment to love the one who gave himself for us in that wonderfully mysterious way. Whatever it is for you – and it may be one or more of these things – it is your opportunity to renew your dedication to him in the company of others who are also called and set apart for his service. It is a means by which we draw nearer to him and nearer to one another as we gather round the table. 'Give us this day our daily bread.'

'Give us, O Lord, more of Jesus Christ, bring him closer to us every day, and feed us on his Word, so that we may truly grow and flourish as your children in the world where you have called us to live and bear witness to the salvation he came to bring in the breaking of his body for our deliverance.'

4. FORGIVE US OUR SINS, AS WE FORGIVE THOSE WHO SIN AGAINST US

Debts, trespasses or sins?

This line of the Lord's Prayer is without any doubt the most difficult of them all. For a start, it is the only one that contains a serious translation problem, and one with which even casual churchgoers are at least vaguely familiar. More importantly, it seems to be making a demand that is not only uncongenial to us but almost impossible to fulfil, even if we want to. How many of us can have much confidence that we have been forgiven by God, once we realize that the measure of that forgiveness appears to be our ability to extend the same forgiveness to others? There is a challenge here that strikes at the heart of our being, revealing both the depths of our own need on the one hand, and of God's love for us on the other.

Let us begin with the translation question first. What exactly is it that we are supposed to be asking forgiveness for – our trespasses, our debts or our sins? All three terms can be found in regular use, and although the general idea is clear, there are subtle differences of nuance among them that make it important to decide what we are talking about. The Greek original is straightforward, at least at first sight. The word used for the things is *opheilēmata* and the people who do them to us are *opheiletai*, words that in normal usage mean 'debts' and 'debtors' respectively. These are the translations found in the Authorized (King James) Version of 1611 and it is interesting to note that they have been used again in the English Standard Version (ESV, 2001), which aims to stay as close to the original text as possible.

The rendering 'trespass' goes back to William Tyndale, the first translator of the Scriptures into modern English, and it was picked up in the Book of Common Prayer, though without acknowledgment. Tyndale's translation of the New Testament is one of the best ever to have been done in English, but as he was an outlaw at the time he never got the recognition he deserved and it fell to others to complete his work later on. By the time the Authorized Version was produced, his translations had become so familiar that it was impossible to dislodge them from the Prayer Book, which was where most people came across the Lord's Prayer in daily use. It is for that reason that 'trespass' has entered our consciousness and remained there, and is probably more familiar than 'debts' to most people today.[1]

The third option is 'sins', which does not occur in any traditional translation but has become popular in recent times. Partly this is because the word is simple and in common use, and it covers the basic meaning of the original, even if Matthew's Greek does not use the equivalent word in this context. The question is complicated because we are dealing with a translation from the original Aramaic (or perhaps even Hebrew) and it is not known what the underlying term being translated was. Both Semitic languages were capable of employing 'debts' to mean 'sins', so Matthew may be giving a totally literal rendering of the original when he uses this term. Interestingly enough, Luke gives 'sins'

1. An exception must be made for Scotland and the Presbyterian tradition, which derives from that country. Not having the Anglican Prayer Book, the Scots used the text of the Authorized Version exclusively, making them more familiar with 'debts' than with 'trespasses'.

(*hamartiai*) for the things but retreats to 'debtors' (*opheiletai*) for the people. This strongly suggests that 'debts' was the original reading. Perhaps Luke thought that its meaning was ambiguous and felt the need to explain the underlying Aramaic term in a clearer way. But he failed to carry this through consistently, perhaps because there was no word meaning 'those who have sinned against us'.[2] For all we know, Jesus may have used two different Aramaic words that Matthew subsequently harmonized into one, but it is clear that whatever happened during the transition from Aramaic to Greek, the concept the Evangelists were dealing with can be accurately conveyed by 'sins' as much as by 'debts' or 'trespasses', and so the modern tendency to prefer that word is not inconsistent with the meaning of the original.

Which of these versions should we prefer? Strict accuracy would dictate that 'debts' is best, even though nowadays most people think of debts primarily in financial terms. When the word is used in a non-financial sense it tends to be in ways that cannot really be regarded as sinful. For example, we often hear people saying things like 'I owe a great debt of gratitude to so-and-so for all the assistance I received,' and so on. The sense of obligation contained in the word 'debt' comes across quite clearly, but no-one would suggest there is anything wrong with this, and the person to whom the debt is owed would certainly not expect to have to forgive someone who makes a remark like that. On the contrary, he or she would probably feel very pleased and even humbled by such a recognition!

There is a further complication in that the Greek text goes on to use the word *paraptōmata* a few verses later, when Jesus is clearly expanding on this statement. As the ESV puts it, 'If you forgive others their trespasses, your heavenly Father will also forgive you, but if you do not forgive others their trespasses, neither will your Father forgive your trespasses' (Matt. 6:14–15). The context makes it clear that *opheilēmata* and *paraptōmata* are synonymous, though whether the latter word is best translated 'trespasses' is less certain.

---

2. There is, of course, a word for 'sinner' (*hamartōlos*), but it is impossible to say 'as we forgive our sinners'!

A trespass, like a transgression, is basically a foot movement. It is literally a walking across or away from the right pathway, a going beyond what is acceptable. This is actually how we use it in normal speech today – a 'No Trespassing' sign means we are forbidden to walk on property that does not belong to us and where there is no public right of way. Such trespassing is against the law, of course, but is generally regarded as a minor infraction that is unlikely to be punished. If it is, most of the time it will probably attract no more than a small fine. To the modern mind, 'forgive us our trespasses' may therefore come across as something like 'overlook our faux pas', which is certainly socially desirable but hardly very serious in moral or spiritual terms. It is rather like treading on somebody's toes – unpleasant for the victim and to be avoided as much as possible, but something that can easily happen by accident, is seldom malicious and ought normally to be excused without further ado.

The Greek *paraptōmata* is more serious than that, not least because it contains the word 'fall'. In secular Greek usage, the word had come to mean a slip or blunder, and was regularly used by ancient accountants to refer to mistakes in their reckoning. If Matthew the tax-collector was the author of the Gospel that circulates under his name, then the use of a financial term like this one would have seemed perfectly natural to him. But *paraptōmata* literally means 'falling away'. Greek-speaking people would easily have sensed an association with the *ptōsis* or fall of Adam, not to mention the *ptōma*, 'a thing that has fallen', or more precisely a dead body or corpse, a meaning which reminds us that the result of sin is death (Rom. 6:23). Unfortunately, no English word conveys this range of ideas precisely, in the way that the German *Verfall* does, for example. It might have been possible at one time to devise an English equivalent (forfall?) but this was not done and it is too late now. The only word in our language that comes remotely close to this idea is 'downfall', but although we might get away with using it in some contexts, it is not a term often found in the plural. By its nature, a 'downfall' tends to be definitive and so we assume it will occur only once – very few people who experience one make such a comeback that they live to do it all over again! But our *paraptōmata* are many and their effects are less immediately catastrophic, so 'downfall' will not do, and 'trespass' is probably as close as we are likely to get to the original sense.

The use of *opheilēmata*, 'debts', may perhaps be explained as a kind of euphemism that frequently occurs when something unpleasant is being talked about. We are familiar with the phenomenon of renaming rubbish tips 'household waste amenity points' or words to that effect, and of course we all know that what were once 'concubines' and 'mistresses' have now become 'partners' in official discourse. Debts may not be altogether desirable, but at least they are more respectable than sins or *paraptōmata*, and the preference shown for the term may have something to do with that. If so, there is no doubt about the real meaning, and surely the translator ought to bring that out rather than obscure it by giving us an overly literal rendering.

To conclude these observations, the recent adoption of the word 'sins' ties in well with the rest of Scripture and is the term we usually end up using when we start talking about this verse in any depth. We have no way of knowing why the Greek did not use *hamartiai* when translating the Aramaic original, but perhaps it has something to do with the fact that *hamartiai* were frequently thought of as ritual sins, failures to keep the law in some way or other, and it was important for Christians not to misunderstand what Jesus was saying. When Jesus told his disciples to ask for forgiveness of their sins, he did not mean that they should be excusing themselves for neglecting the finer points of ritual purity. He was not concerned with that at all. Indeed, in that respect he was himself regarded as a great sinner, because he refused to be bound by the niceties of Jewish convention. This is speculation, but as a possible explanation it makes sense in the context and may give us a better idea of how the minds of first-century Jewish Christians worked. But whatever the truth of the matter is, it is clear that in the Lord's Prayer the Greek words *opheilēmata* and *paraptōmata* mean what we today would normally call 'sins', and even if we retain words like 'debts' or 'trespasses' for the sake of familiarity, it is basically sins we are talking about.

Forgive us our sins

What then are sins? Like many words in common use, we think we know the answer, but it takes careful analysis to see whether we have really grasped the full significance of the word. In common parlance today, we may still come across the phrase 'living in sin' as a euphemism for cohabitation outside marriage, though now that this is much more common than it used to be, the expression is beginning to sound a little quaint. But the popular association of sin with sexual impropriety is still strong, as anyone who reads the tabloid press will quickly realize. Another area in which the word has a certain currency is that of diet – chocolate cake, for instance, may be described as having a sinful amount of calories, though it seems a trifle unfair to shift the blame on to calories when they are not the ones who have done anything wrong! Oddly enough, both of these associations can claim some sort of scriptural backing. After all, it was through eating the forbidden fruit that Adam and Eve fell from grace, and it was only then that they began to feel shame at their nakedness, a reaction that is usually assumed to mean that they became embarrassed by their sexuality. Such mental links can have an extraordinarily long life, but it would be quite wrong to limit the scope of sin to gluttony and lust. Even the medieval theologians who studied the matter in great detail came up with five other deadly sins, and the worst of them was neither of these, but pride. Clearly, there is more to the question of sin than meets the eyes of most people, and we need to look very carefully at it before going on to consider what it means to have these sins of ours forgiven.

The first thing that has to be said about sin is that it is not a natural human activity and was not intended as such by God. When God created human beings, he did so in order for them to be fruitful and multiply, and fill the earth. He gave them dominion over the other creatures and the right to till the ground. He did not create them with the intention that they should sin, and nothing in the material universe would have led them into sin. The Bible is very clear about this. When God created the world, he looked at it and saw that it was very good (Gen. 1:31). Unfortunately, in the time of Jesus that perception had been compromised in two different but ultimately complementary ways. From as far back as the time of Moses, Jews had been given food laws that divided the world into things that were 'clean' and 'unclean'. They were forbidden to eat camels or ostriches (Lev. 11:4, 16), but most of them understood that this did not mean that camels and ostriches were evil in themselves, because everything God had created was essentially good, whether it could be eaten or not. But many pious Jews had come to believe that anyone who ate such things, or who ate lawfully prescribed food in the wrong way (or in the wrong company) defiled themselves by doing so. By giving ritual commands a moral dimension, these Jews had fallen into an error that became particularly serious when it was extended to cover human beings who did not conform to the prescribed rituals. The result, as we can see from the Gospels, was that in the eyes of many Jewish religious leaders, sin had become a matter of outward religious nonconformity and had almost entirely lost its spiritual dimension. This is why Jesus had to remind them that evil did not come from the food they ate but from the thoughts and intentions of their hearts – something that should have been obvious but had become badly obscured by this false interpretation of the law of Moses (Matt. 15:17–20).

In the Gentile world, on the other hand, the dualistic philosophies of ancient Greece had taken over the intellectual elites, who had come to believe that anything material was automatically evil. To their minds, only spiritual realities could be good, and in their understanding salvation meant escaping from the body and returning to the realm of pure spirit. Those who wanted that salvation were therefore obliged to practise a severe form of asceticism in this life, because that was as close as they could get to doing without material things altogether. Christianity tackled this belief head-on and it was one of the main reasons why the philosophers of ancient Greece remained the last hold-out of ancient paganism, despite their disdain for Greek mythology.[3] Not merely the creation of the world by a good and loving God, but also the incarnation of his Son and the resurrection of the body as well as the spirit all pointed in the same direction – the material

---

3. The philosophical schools of Athens were finally closed in 529, two hundred years after the legalization of Christianity. By that time they had become a cultural anomaly, representing something that had long since faded out of popular consciousness.

creation was a good thing and it took part, along with the spiritual, in the redemptive plan of God. Today we have officially abandoned this ancient Greek attitude and most people have a much more positive approach to material things – perhaps even too positive in many cases. But the tendency to promote asceticism is always there and resurfaces from time to time. Rich and overweight people in the developed world can often be persuaded to feel guilty about this, and rightly so in some cases, but the idea that possessions are a bad thing in themselves and ought to be renounced cannot be the answer for everyone. Perhaps God does call some people to go that far, and if so, fine. But for most of us it is not the renunciation of what we have been given, but the right use of it that is the thing we have to concentrate on.

This may sound easier, but it is actually much more difficult because it forces us to make judgments about things that a complete renunciation of them would not require. As Christians, we are responsible to God for what he has given us, and if we just throw it away we are effectively rejecting that responsibility. The great Scottish-American philanthropist Andrew Carnegie said that it was a disgrace to die rich, but he did not mean by this that he should simply throw his wealth away. On the contrary, he made very careful use of it in establishing charities and public amenities that continue to fulfil important social functions to this day. He was a man who appreciated the value of material things and used them for what they were worth, not a guilt-ridden Midas who ran away from his opportunity to use what had been given to him for the greater good of humanity. Not all of us have the resources of Andrew Carnegie, but that is not the point. What matters is that we should accept that our disposable income belongs to God and that for us to use it responsibly means using it for his glory.

Sin and evil are present in the world but although God allows them to exist, he did not create them or desire them to come into being. In fact, nothing that God created is evil in itself, not even Satan. Evil is not a substantial quality but the fruit of rebellion – disobedience to the will of God. God did not make us that way, but on the other hand he did create us with the freedom to choose, and it is a fact of history that our first parents chose to rebel against him. You may say, 'I did not make this choice, I have inherited sin from Adam whether I like it or not, so why does the Christian faith teach that I am to be held accountable for something that is not my fault? How fair is that?' The argument is an old one, and was answered by the apostle Paul who said:

> Who are you, O man, to answer back to God? Will what is moulded say
> to its moulder, 'Why have you made me like this?' Has the potter no
> right over the clay . . .? What if God, desiring to show his wrath and to
> make known his power, has endured with much patience vessels of
> wrath prepared for destruction, in order to make known the riches of
> his glory for vessels of mercy, which he has prepared beforehand for
> glory . . .? (Rom. 9:20–23)

It is true, of course, that as human beings we have inherited our sinfulness from others and are not directly responsible for it in the way Adam was. But we have to remember that that is also true of everything else about us too. For example, I did not choose when and where to be born, I did not pick my parents, my sex, my height, my skin colour, my nationality, my education . . . I could go on and on. Almost everything about me comes from somewhere outside myself and was given to me regardless of what I might think about it. When I was living in Africa, I very much wished that I had been born black, because then I could blend into my surroundings and not stand out as the only white person in the village. Perhaps I felt an added twinge of postcolonial guilt, and was certainly aware that white people in Africa were expected to have a higher standard of living because of that colonial past that had taken them there as a dominant caste in the first place. I realized then that I could not simply accept what was good about my human inheritance and reject the rest: if I have benefited from my ancestors' good points, I also have to suffer the consequences of their bad behaviour. I can honestly say that no-one ever blamed me personally for the sins of the white race in Africa but I could not escape or ignore that legacy and did my best to ensure that my own behaviour did not add another sorry chapter to the saga.

On a more individual level, I am glad to say that neither of my parents ever smoked or took drugs, but if they had and if that had affected me in the womb, I could not now choose to disregard the consequences, but would have to live with them. We are not the totally free agents we sometimes imagine ourselves to be, and when it comes to sin we are not free at all. We have inherited it because our first parents went wrong and now we have to live with the consequences. Having said that, sin is not part of our 'nature' in the sense that it was not created by God and implanted in us from the beginning. As we have already seen, when God made Adam and Eve he saw that they were very good, and so whatever sin is, it cannot be regarded as a defect in their created nature. Here we have to remember that when the Bible speaks about human nature, it is almost always referring to our physical being, which may be weak and may have been badly affected by the fall, but which is not evil in itself. Adam and Eve were mortal beings who were protected from death in the Garden of Eden, but when they fell from grace that protection was removed so that they died. Had they been immortal beings, like the angels, they would still have fallen from grace but would not have perished, just as Satan and his hosts lost their exalted position but continue to exist as beings in their own right. This is the difference between sinfulness and mortality, and we must be very careful not to say that our physical natures are sinful just because they are mortal.

The justice of God

It is important to remind ourselves of this because there have always been people who have assumed that physical handicaps or illnesses have something to do with sin. For centuries it was believed that mentally ill people were possessed by the devil and they were appallingly badly treated because of that. It is true that the New Testament gives several examples of people who were possessed by demons and exhibited the outward signs of mental illness, so those who perceived a connection between the two things were not entirely to blame for this, but they cannot be simply equated with one other. Today very few people would connect them and we have been set free to treat mental illnesses as they should be treated. This is a great blessing, but unfortunately it seems as though we may now have fallen into the opposite trap and been encouraged to suppose that demon possession is entirely fictitious. That is going too far in the other direction, and we must be grateful that there are spiritually gifted exorcists in the church who have been given the gift of discernment and who know what must be done to cast the evil spirits out. As long as we remember that although physical illness is not by itself proof of an underlying spiritual problem, such a problem may be present, we are unlikely to go seriously wrong.

On another front, there are some Christians who seem to think that they have a right to health, wealth and a long life simply because they are believers. This so-called 'prosperity gospel' has made great inroads in recent years, particularly among disadvantaged people in the developing world who are easily attracted by the promise of a better life. However, it is a false and pernicious doctrine that has to be resisted because it can lead only to disillusionment and loss of faith when the so-called 'promises' fail to materialize. Of course, it is true that our physical circumstances can be affected by our spiritual attitudes and behaviour (usually for the worse, it must be said) but this is not invariably the case and we cannot make a one-to-one correspondence between them. The story of Job exists to make this point, and we would do well to take it to heart. Its author goes to great pains to insist that Job was a righteous man who had done nothing to offend God, and that God was in no way displeased with him. The question nevertheless arose as to whether Job's faith in God was due to his good fortune. Would he be quite so loyal to his Creator if things started to go badly wrong for him? Satan thought that Job would change his tune pretty quickly if his circumstances changed for the worse, but God trusted him and told Satan that he was wrong to think that. In order to demonstrate the point, God allowed Satan to afflict Job in various ways to see what the result would be.

As we know, Job passed the test with flying colours. The most depressing thing about his story is not the number and range of the troubles he had to face, great though they undoubtedly were, but the reaction of his family and friends to his misfortune. His wife was so annoyed that she simply wanted him to curse God and be done with it (Job 2:9). The friends who turned up to comfort him turned out to be more trouble than they were worth. Job ended up defending himself against them and pointing out that his willingness to submit to God was not an admission of some secret guilt which he did not have, but an acceptance that God has a right to do as he pleases and that Job's place was to accept that and trust him to know what he was up to, even if this was not clear to anyone else. It is important to notice that although the author states quite clearly that Job's sufferings came from Satan (by divine permission), Job himself betrays no knowledge of this. He never blames the devil for his misfortunes, but regards everything that happens to him as coming from God. In other words, there is no underlying dualism in his thinking. For Job, 'good' and 'evil' come from the same source, and it is to that source that he looks for his salvation (Job 19:25). In the end, God reveals himself to Job and commends him for his faithfulness by rewarding him more richly than he was rewarded before his troubles started. But God never suggests to Job that he was not responsible for everything that occurred, and never mentions Satan's role at all. The final message is that God is sovereign over all creation, and that no human being, however upright and faithful he may be, has any right to question what the divine ruler of the universe has decreed.

Whether Job was a historical figure may be doubted, but it scarcely matters. The story has become a classic of biblical literature because it is universally recognized as being true to life. The world is still full of people who bear their sufferings without complaining, but who are surrounded by sympathizers who are always looking for someone else to blame. It is still true that good people often seem to be singled out for trouble, whereas the openly wicked are allowed to flaunt their evil doings any way they can. Psalm 73 explores this mystery, because the psalmist saw clearly that there was no correspondence between prosperity and goodness. What he could not figure out was why the wicked prospered and the good suffered. God did not give him a direct answer to his question any more than he explained everything to Job, but he did make it clear that it would all work out for the best in the end. Prosperity in this world is for a time only, and those who have enjoyed earthly success without deserving it will reap their reward after death. As Jesus pointed out, the ungodly rich man will languish in hell while the godly but poor Lazarus will spend eternity in Abraham's bosom, close to the throne of God (Luke 16:20–25). That is the perspective God wants us to adopt when we find ourselves confronted by such apparent anomalies. They test our faith, to be sure, but if our faith is securely anchored in heaven we shall have nothing to fear, because we shall be safe in the hand of God.

Another common error many people make is to suppose that sin and evil are merely the absence of good. The theory here is that because everything created is good, evil cannot exist as such and must be understood as a deprivation. Important and influential people like St Augustine have believed this, and it is still possible to find traces of it today. For example, the late Karl Barth refused to accept that Satan could be a person because in his mind personhood was a positive thing. Therefore, to be wicked was to be deprived of personhood, or at least aspects of it. Whatever evil was, it could not be defined in personal terms, in spite of the very clear indication in the Bible that Satan has strong personal characteristics and interacts with both God and man. As the Bible explains it, sin originated as a personal act of rebellion by Satan against God. He was the first one to disobey the will of his Creator and was fully conscious of what he was doing. We can only speculate about what his motive may have been, but theologians have traditionally ascribed it to pride – Satan wanted to claim equality with God and control his own life. It is hard to imagine what else could have motivated him, and the fact that the suggestion ties in remarkably well with what he promised Adam and Eve, when he offered them the chance to eat of the fruit of the tree of the knowledge of good and evil, reinforces the likelihood that it was indeed something like this that drove him to rebellion in the first place.

By doing what Satan suggested, Adam and Eve would acquire the divine ability to make moral judgments they did not yet possess, and to that extent they would become more like God than they already were. What they did not realize, until it was too late, was that by acceding to the will of Satan they were being trapped by him. The gift they would receive would turn out to condemn them and cut them off from God, rather than drawing them closer to him as Satan had originally promised. Fallen human beings can take moral decisions, but whatever we decide to do is tainted by the fact that we are in a broken relationship with God. As a result, even if we decide to do the right thing, it is still wrong in God's eyes, because the foundation of the relationship he wants to have with us has been destroyed. As Article XIII of the Thirty-Nine Articles tells us, works done before justification 'partake of the nature of sin' however good they may be in themselves, because they are performed by people who have not been born again by the Spirit of God. To put it simply, good works can be done only by good people, and good people do not exist!

That may be hard for some of us to swallow but at least it is logical. You shall know a tree by its fruit, says the Bible, and if the tree is unhealthy it is unlikely that the fruit will be any different, even if it appears to look good on the surface (Matt. 12:33). More problematic is the present situation of believers in Christ. If we have been cleansed from our sins by his blood and born again into a new and eternal life by his Spirit, how is it that we still go on sinning? Where do these sins come from and what can we do about them? In the early church, it was often thought that the sinfulness we are born with, what theologians call 'original sin', was washed away by baptism, along with every other sin we might have committed up to then. The snag was that once baptism was administered, it could not be repeated, so that anyone who sinned after being baptized was automatically condemned to hell. The only way out of this dire fate was to die for Christ, to receive what was known as the baptism of fire, or martyrdom.[4] This was often a very real option in the early centuries of the church, but even so, it was extremely hard on people who were presented with so unenviable a choice. As a result, more and more Christians decided to defer their baptism until they were on the point of death and unlikely to commit further sins. It must have been tough for those who recovered from what they had thought was their terminal illness, but despite the risk of that, the practice of deathbed baptism was thought to be the best option, even though it clearly went against the teaching of the New Testament on the subject.

---

4. This idea was based on Jesus' words in Luke 12:49–53. See also 1 Cor. 3:10–15.

Eventually, it was decided that although baptism washed away original sin, it did not affect post-baptismal sins one way or the other. On the one hand, this meant that baptized people who went on sinning involuntarily would not lose their salvation as long as they adhered to the other sacraments of the church, which provided a remedy for the problem of post-baptismal sin. But even regular and diligent use of the sacraments was not enough to deal with the immense weight of human sin, and apart from a very few people who somehow managed to live the kind of life God demanded and so did not fall into his debt as a result of their sinfulness, most people continued to need further cleansing after death before they could hope to enter the kingdom of heaven. Could such cleansing be provided? There was nothing in the New Testament or in the teaching of the early church to suggest that it could, but it seemed grossly unfair that there would be large numbers of people who ended up in hell despite the fact that they had been earnestly trying all their lives to get to heaven. Surely, there had to be some divine mercy that would help these people achieve their goal after death! Thus was born the idea of 'purgatory', a place invented by the medieval church as a means of providing relief and assurance to sinners who knew they were not good enough to go straight to heaven but felt that their faith ought to be sufficient to keep them out of hell.

The invention of purgatory was a brilliant solution to the problem of post-baptismal sin. It got even better when the church came up with the idea that it was possible to have the time people spent there reduced, not so much for good behaviour on their part as because of the intercessions of those whom they had left behind on earth. Time off in purgatory was known as an 'indulgence' in theological terms, and people could perform meritorious acts of piety on earth in order to earn indulgences for dead relatives and others who were in purgatory, or even for themselves in the future. Performing such acts was often inconvenient, however, and so the church came up with the ingenious solution of *selling* indulgences. This spared the buyer the need to do anything time-consuming or embarrassing, and it benefited the church, which would far rather have lots of money than see thousands of

penitents doing things like beat themselves with rods or walk bare-
foot in the snow, to no evident practical purpose.

Historians of the church know that it was the indiscriminate
sale of indulgences that lit the fuse which sparked off the
Protestant reformation. How was it possible, said Martin Luther,
to purchase the grace of God? How could someone have his sins
forgiven when he showed not the slightest sign of repentance, but
had only a large purse with which to buy off his accusers? Just as
today people in a tight spot are often willing to offer hush money
to those who might expose and embarrass them, so many
medieval people were quite prepared to buy off the church, which
they saw as a way of keeping God on their side. Even now it is not
unknown for non-churchgoers to offer the occasional donation,
especially after a funeral, in the hope that God will put a good
word in for them if they ever need it, so we should not be surprised at how popular the sale of indulgences turned out to be.

The sale of indulgences was a scandal, but Martin Luther would
not have made any lasting impression on the church if all he had
done was to criticize that. Others had done the same thing before
him but had got nowhere, because the abuse of a system does not
mean that the system itself is necessarily wrong. To this day, there
are Roman Catholic apologists who are prepared to agree that the
people Luther was objecting to had gone too far and that he was
right to protest against their behaviour, but they insist that he fell
into error when he began to question the system itself. If only
Luther had stuck to the level of a reformer of abuses, they claim,
he would now be a saint of the church and the Reformation that
split Western Christendom in two would never have occurred.

This is an attractive thesis, but it ignores the fact that the system
of indulgences rested on a shaky foundation that had little to do
with the practice of selling them. Even if indulgences had been
given away, or if people had been forced to earn them by serious
acts of penance, the system would still have been wrong, because
the understanding of sin and forgiveness that lay behind it was
fundamentally mistaken. The basic flaw in it was that the medieval
church believed that sacramental acts like baptism had the power
to take away sin. Once that idea took root, the only real question
was how that power should be used. This had produced a complex

system of confession, penance and absolution, all of which were administered by the priest on behalf of the church to those who conformed to its wishes.

The key to understanding the Protestant revolution lies in the way in which we interpret the word 'penance'. In Latin this word is *poenitentia*, and it can be translated three different ways in English – 'penance', 'penitence' and 'repentance'. This variety of possible translations is not an accident, nor are the three English words synonymous. On the contrary, they reflect the disputes that divided the sixteenth-century church and that still shape the expression of our faith today.

What we call 'penance' was a sacrament of the church and had been well worked out in medieval theology. It could be quantified according to the gravity of the sin committed and it was the job of the priest to work out the appropriate calculation. You killed your mother-in-law? That means sixteen 'Hail Marys' on bended knee, preferably on each step of the church of Scala Coeli in Rome, or some other suitable venue. You kicked the bishop's horse? Twenty 'Hail Marys'. And so on. I am caricaturing this of course, but only to bring out more clearly the underlying point, which remains valid. There was a scale of sins divided into the basic categories of 'venial', which did not incur the risk of being eternally damned, and 'mortal', which did. To be caught at death with venial sins that had not been confessed would mean no more than a few extra millennia in purgatory, but if there were mortal sins outstanding, the impenitent sinner would go straight to hell. Hence the near panic when a person was on the point of death. If he did not confess and receive the last rights from the priest in time, there was a real risk that his soul might be lost for eternity.

Luther came to understand that *poenitentia* was not meant to be a series of external acts corresponding to the supposed seriousness of particular sins, but an inner attitude of heart and mind – what we now call 'repentance'. This discovery turned Protestantism into a form of Christianity different from medieval Catholicism, and ensured that the Reformation would not just be a transient clean-up operation. As we might expect, Luther's opponents argued that penance and repentance were two sides of the same coin; in their view, the outward signs were never meant to be separated from the inward spiritual state. This may have been true in theory, but in practice it did not work out that way. As time went on, Luther developed his teaching on repentance to the point where he thought it was best simply to drop the outward practices we collectively know as 'penance', and he abandoned his earlier belief that this was a sacrament on a par with baptism and Holy Communion. As a result, the entire confessional system of the medieval church was replaced by something quite different. What was that?

Justification by faith alone

As Luther read the New Testament, he came to see that the only basis for forgiveness of sins was the justification that comes by faith in Jesus Christ. This faith is not a matter of doing things, but of trusting that Christ has already done what we cannot do for ourselves. That is the key. No matter how hard we try, no matter how many years we spend in purgatory, we can never pay the price for our sins. In other words, we can never do enough to earn our forgiveness. Sin is too deep, too radical, too serious, to be disposed of in that way. Only a work of God is capable of getting to grips with it, and that work was fully accomplished by Christ on the cross. Our lives do not and cannot change for the better; we are sinners to the day we die, and to pretend otherwise is merely to deceive ourselves. But this does not mean that we are irredeemably lost, because Christ has taken our place on the cross, paid the debt we owe to God and covered us with his righteousness. We are therefore able to stand in the presence of our heavenly Father, not boasting of any righteousness of our own but trusting completely in the righteousness of Christ that has been made available, or as theologians say, has been 'imputed' to us.

Once belief in the imputation of Christ's righteousness took root, it made the traditional system of works for time off in purgatory meaningless in itself and blasphemous in relation to God. If Jesus has done all that is needed, how can we presume to add to his work by inventions of our own? But once our works cease to have any value, faith becomes all important. Without it, Christ's righteousness cannot be imputed to us and we shall not be covered by it on the Day of Judgment. Failing to trust in him for our salvation means full exposure to the wrath of God when the final reckoning comes. For all these reasons, justification by faith, and by faith alone, makes the difference between 'a standing and a falling church', to use the traditional expression. One of the objections to this doctrine is that it appears to turn faith itself into a work. You may not have to make a pilgrimage to Rome to be saved, but if working your way into a confession of faith is what is demanded instead, is that not just as arduous and demanding? Perhaps even more so, you might think!

Is it true that in proclaiming justification by faith alone, Protestants have merely exchanged one kind of work for another? Here there is a serious misunderstanding about the nature of faith that needs to be addressed because it is so widespread. Justifying faith is not to be confused either with the act or with the content of believing, important as both of those things are. In fact, both the act of believing and mental assent to a confession of faith are the result of justification, and not its cause. It is because we have been justified that we are led to believe certain things in a particular way. The creeds and confessions of the church are not examinations we have to pass in order to get into the kingdom of heaven, but witnesses to what we have already met and experienced in Christ. But if these statements of belief are not the faith that justifies, what is such a faith?

The key to understanding justifying faith is to realize that it is a gift of God. The apostle Paul states this quite clearly when he writes, 'By the grace given to me I say to everyone among you not to think of himself more highly that he ought to think, but to think with sober judgment, each according to the measure of faith that God has assigned' (Rom. 12:3). There is no question here of any sort of human merit. To think of oneself with 'sober judgment' is to realize that having done everything in the service of Christ, we remain unprofitable servants, entitled to nothing and dependent as ever on God's mercy for our salvation (Luke 17:10). To those who lack this justifying faith it all sounds depressing and incredible. Everything in the human mind cries out for 'fairness' and 'justice' and it seems outrageous that good works will have no reward. But those who have experienced the power of justifying faith at work in their lives have been set free from such delusions. They have come to understand that there is no such thing as 'fairness' or 'justice', or if there is, they can only lead to our condemnation. We have been rescued from that – most 'unfairly' and 'unjustly' we might add! God has reached into our lives and we are now his children (Gal. 4:6). Why he should have reconciled me to himself in this way I do not know – this is the peace of God that passes all understanding (Phil. 4:7). I have done nothing to obtain it, and mercifully I can do nothing to lose it again either, much as I sometimes try to do so. I am completely unworthy of it and would not have it at all if God had not decided to give it to me. There indeed is the mystery, or the scandal if you prefer, of salvation. Here am I, holding the treasure of justifying faith in an earthen vessel unfit to contain it (2 Cor. 4:7), appointed by God to be a light to the world whether I want to be or not, and destined by him to dwell in heaven for eternity when I have never even been there before. All my righteousness is as filthy rags (Isa. 64:6), but he has put a crown on my head and covered me with the royal robes of heaven. That is my justification, and when I turn from it to look at myself, I am driven back to God, who has shown me what I am in myself, and, more important still, what I am to become in him. That is justifying faith; that is why I have been saved. My sin is still with me, but something greater has come into my life and taken away its power, so that the life I now live is no longer my own, but the life of Christ, the righteous One who dwells in me by his Spirit.

The imputation of Christ's righteousness to us as sinners and the presence of this justifying faith in our lives does not mean that we cease to sin. Luther's great discovery was that once we are under Christ's protection, sin does not disappear, but it no longer counts against us. Thanks to him we are now justified sinners, or, as the Latin tag puts it, a Christian is *simul iustus et peccator* (at the same time righteous and a sinner). This was a radically new concept to the people of the early sixteenth century and for many of them it was totally unacceptable. In their minds, justification before God was inextricably linked to sanctification, so much so that the two terms were often regarded as no more than different ways of looking at the same thing. Sanctification was seen in a

changed life, in works of piety which demonstrated to the whole
world that the person concerned meant what he or she said. Many
people gave very generously of their time and money to establish
hospitals, schools, orphanages and the like as proof that they were
really children of God. Some directed their resources to what we
today might think were more dubious causes, as King Henry VI
did, who built King's College chapel in Cambridge so that prayers
could be said there daily for the repose of his soul after his death,
but no-one could question their zeal or their sincerity. In a few
cases, there were people whose dedication to the works of
sanctification was so great that they became completely identified
with them, and people believed that God worked through them
(sometimes well after their death) to perform miracles. These were
the 'saints' whose memory is still preserved in churches and
chapels all over the world.

Luther's reformation changed all that. To his mind, anyone who
was justified by faith was a saint already, and in this respect he had
the usage of the New Testament, and especially of the apostle
Paul, on his side.[5] But these saints were clearly sinners too, since if
they were not, Paul would not have had to write to them. How was
such a contradiction possible? Surely, it must be the case that the
holier a person is, the less he or she will sin! One of the things
Protestants often fail to appreciate is that their critics, especially
those in the Roman Catholic Church, find it very hard to understand how we can reject what they see as an obvious equation.
How can we be convinced we are going to heaven and yet go on
sinning? Is it really possible to make a profession of faith and then
do nothing to change our lives, without any danger of losing our
salvation?

Protestants, of course, do not follow this line of argument, and
if they understand it at all, they see it as a caricature of what
Luther and his followers really taught. Faith in Christ is much
more than belief in an intellectual sense; it is nothing less than
union with him. The Bible describes this as being ingrafted into

---

5. Among the numerous passages that could be cited, cf. Rom. 15:25; 1 Cor.
14:33; 2 Cor. 1:1; Phil. 4:22.

him so that his life becomes our life and his righteousness becomes our righteousness (Rom. 11:17–24). We are like branches of an olive tree, bearing fruit because we are solidly fixed to the trunk and incapable of doing anything by ourselves. It is the trunk that gives life to the branches; they can be cut off but the trunk must remain and continue its nourishing work if the tree is to survive. But just as it is sometimes the case that branches start to decay and have to be pruned if they are to go on bearing fruit, so it is true that believers in Christ are not made perfect simply by being united with him. We are still in Adam, and as long as this is so we are still sinners in need of forgiveness. What has changed is the basis on which that forgiveness is offered and the meaning attached to it. It is to this great question of forgiveness that we must now turn, because God's forgiveness is ultimately even more fundamental than justifying faith. After all, if he had not forgiven us first, there would be nothing for us to put our faith in!

Forgiveness is offered to us on the basis of what Christ has done for us and not what we have done for ourselves. As a Christian, the Holy Spirit convicts me of my need to repent for the sins I commit daily. I have a finite mind and so can never fully comprehend the extent of my sins, but whether I know about them or not, I believe they have been forgiven in Christ. What I have to do is receive that forgiveness and understand what it means for me. Receiving forgiveness sounds as if it ought to be easy but in fact often it is not. One of the main reasons for this is that we are proud people and do not like to feel that we are totally dependent on others, not even on God. There is something in us that does not want free forgiveness, and if we need to be pardoned for some reason, we would rather earn it or pay for it in some way. Call this self-respect if you will, or pride – however you express it, it is there and acts as a barrier to growth in my relationship with God. But unless and until we surrender totally to him and accept his will for us, we cannot receive his forgiveness and it will have no effect on our lives.

Then too, some people are convinced they have sinned so badly in their lives that they can never be forgiven. Such people cannot forgive themselves for what they have done, and so they find it impossible to accept that God could ever forgive them either.

Sometimes they are victims of a false modesty, thinking that God could not possibly be concerned with anyone as unimportant as they are. The notion that the Son of God should have left his heavenly throne in order to die for them seems so absurdly disproportionate that they refuse to accept it is true. Why should the ruler of the universe bother with the likes of them? Behind this kind of thinking often lurks a hidden fear. People do not want to be forgiven, because in a curious way it deprives them of their identity and security. It may not be very pleasant to have to live with our sins, but if we know what they are, they can be surprisingly comforting. They give us something to concentrate our emotional energies on and protect us from having to look beyond ourselves. Huddling behind our barriers may be uncomfortable at times, but letting those barriers down might expose us to all kinds of unknown dangers. Better the devil we know, we think, and so we fail to reach out in faith to receive something that will change us in new and unsettling ways.

There are also plenty of people who refuse to believe they have done anything seriously wrong. They see no need for forgiveness, and so do not bother to ask for it. For them 'forgive us our sins' is something meant for other people, either because in their minds they have already 'been there and done that' or because they honestly think they have never done anything bad enough to require repentance. Safe in the sheepfold as they suppose they are, they think that such a message is meant for someone who has gone astray and not for them, and so delude themselves into a false security which is the very opposite of saving faith. Such people rarely if ever think they are perfect, and may well be prepared to apologize from time to time if something they have said or done has inadvertently offended someone else. But that is a far cry from true repentance. People who think like that are like the rich young ruler in the Gospel (Matt. 19:16–22). They have never killed anybody, never stolen anything, never committed adultery. They go to church on Sundays, they do not swear, they do not lie about other people and of course they would never dream of making an idol to worship in place of the true God. But it is precisely for these reasons that they fail to see that they have any need of repentance. After all, what have they done wrong? The most they might be guilty of is failing to turn up to some event or sleeping late one Sunday and missing church. But then, as we all agree, nobody is perfect, and does anyone really think they are likely to spend eternity in hell because of something as minor as that? From their perspective of course, these people are quite right to think the way they do, and we should have every sympathy with them.

The trouble is that their thinking is seriously misplaced. By the standards of his time, Jesus was relatively unconcerned about what people did. When he spoke to publicans, prostitutes and politicians he was remarkably forgiving of their behaviour, even when public sentiment was very much against that. It often seems it was only when he came up against the respectable pillars of society that he vented his wrath against them, accusing them of hypocrisy by reducing the demands of the law to a set of rules and ignoring the spiritual principles that undergirded it. Ultimately, Jesus was less bothered about what people did than about the way they thought. Hatred in their hearts towards another person was just as bad as murder – in fact, it *was* murder (Matt. 5:21–26). And it is here that those who think they have no need of forgiveness are often the worst offenders of all. There are many people whose outward lives appear to be models of middle-class respectability, but who are secretly capable of the most dastardly behaviour towards others, particularly those whom they perceive to be a threat to themselves. Furthermore, they often see nothing wrong with this, and may even tell themselves that, unpleasant though the business is, they are doing the world a necessary favour by blocking the career of someone whose influence on it would only be negative. The last thing they would ever consider is the idea that they might be in exactly the same situation themselves!

For Christians, the plea for the forgiveness of our sins is ultimately a plea for a closer walk with God. As we go on in the Christian life our assurance of his loving care grows deeper, but so do does our sorrow and frustration at all the things we do that offend him. The deep-rooted sinfulness that dominates our earthly being becomes increasingly intolerable as we learn more about Christ and draw nearer to him. The more we long to be like him, to spend time with him, to imitate him and to enjoy him, the more we feel that our sins keep dragging us down. The more we sense God's presence in our lives, the more embarrassed we are to look at ourselves. Nothing in our lives is ready for him to come into them, and yet in spite of everything we do that would drive him away, he still turns up and makes his presence felt. When we read the lives of great Christian saints the story is always the same. As the apostle Paul put it towards the end of his earthly ministry, 'To me, though I am the very least of all the saints, this grace was given, to preach to the Gentiles the unsearchable riches of Christ' (Eph. 3:8). Yet near the beginning of that same ministry he had already declared, 'I have been crucified with Christ. It is no longer I who live, but Christ who lives in me' (Gal. 2:20). It is always the same – less of self and more of him as we approach the goal of the heavenly kingdom. But the less of self there is, the more there must be of God's forgiving presence and power at work in us to fill up the void our pride has left behind. To grow in Christ is to become ever more dependent on that forgiveness, which is the true foundation of our new life in him.

When we pray for the forgiveness of our sins, we are praying to receive something already stored up for us in that kingdom. Christ does not have to die a second time, and neither do we have to be born again twice over. The fundamentals of our relationship with God are established, and since this is based on the forgiveness of our sins, we know that there would be no relationship at all between us if that were not already present and active in our experience. But at the same time, our relationship with God is a living thing. Just as we sin every day even after we are converted, so we have to go back to God in humility and ask him yet again to apply his forgiveness to those fresh sins, along with all the others we have previously committed. More importantly, we need to go on asking forgiveness for our sinfulness, which leads to the particular sins we commit and is far more dangerous and all-pervasive than anything we might actually do. I have every confidence that God will continue to forgive me in the future as he has always done in the past, but fearing that he might change his mind is not the problem. What matters is that I should stay in the right relationship with God, and that relationship cannot be disturbed or clouded by any lingering, unconfessed sin.

This is a far more serious spiritual problem than many of us are prepared to recognize. It is difficult to come to terms with this, because unconfessed sin is likely to be unacknowledged and therefore unrecognized. We cannot grapple with something if we do not know it is there, and if things seem to be going along quite well on the surface, there is little incentive to go exploring the inner depths of our being in order to stir up potential trouble. But we need to remember that we are conscious of only a tiny part of ourselves. So much of what we think, say and do springs from hidden parts of our being that only God understands (Ps. 139:1–6). It does not come naturally to us to ask him to forgive us at this level, because we do not know what we are talking about when we do. The only answer is to recognize that there is much that we can never know about ourselves, and to ask God to work in us at those depths that escape our awareness. That he does so is certain, because every so often we realize we have been changed without recognizing it. We no longer react in quite the same way to certain things. We no longer spring to judgment when we meet some familiar shibboleth; we find ourselves talking to people we previously thought we would never be able to put up with; we even find ourselves volunteering to help out when that would never have crossed our minds before. It is then we realize that God has been at work in those hidden depths of our lives, and that the fruits of that work have finally penetrated to the surface where we can recognize and embrace them as the gift of his blessing to us.

Speaking for myself, I have come to the point in my life now where I cannot pray to God at all without pleading for forgiveness, because I am conscious of how far away from him I really am in my own heart and mind. I do not despair of this, because I also know that the closer I get to him the more acutely I shall feel that way. You may think that an experienced preacher and teacher would not have to worry about such things, but the truth is that I am daily more aware of how subtle my sinfulness is. I am afraid of saying the wrong thing, of creating a bad impression, of not being liked, of causing offence to people that will come back to haunt me later on and so on. I tell myself it does not matter whether anyone is listening or not, but in my heart I crave for acceptance and people's praise, and feel hurt if there is none. Yet in the New Testament we read that when Jesus healed ten lepers, only one returned to give him thanks. The other nine simply disappeared (Luke 17:11–19). Is it any different today? Is it not possible, even likely, that many of the people we minister to are people we never speak to, people we know little or nothing about, people who would never dream of approaching us and telling us how much what we have said or done means to them? It may well be so, but in our sinful humanity we long for the nine to come back like the one and wonder what we have done to drive them away, or indeed, if they are really there at all.

Sin is very deep and very subtle, but let us remember that forgiveness is deeper still. Many times I feel that God is making me aware of sins in my life mainly in order to show me just how powerful his forgiveness is. It is almost as if he is saying to me, 'You see, I am greater than you thought I was, because I have even forgiven that sin you thought I knew nothing about!' When that happens I laugh a little at my incorrigible unbelief and reply, 'OK, God. You win yet again. How long is this going to go on?' And the answer comes back loud and clear: 'Until the day I come for you to dwell with me for ever in my kingdom.' Only then will our sinful lives be truly over, and only then will the full blessing of his forgiveness be fully apparent to our eyes.

As we forgive those who sin against us

The petition for the forgiveness of our sins comes with a rider that is surely one of the most challenging lines in the entire Bible: 'As we forgive those who sin against us.' I cannot speak for others, but I have to admit that whenever I think about that I am inclined to feel that I have lost my salvation already. How exactly do I forgive other people who have sinned against me? It is a frightening question, but Jesus not only puts it in the Lord's Prayer, he goes on to discuss the matter further in the verses immediately following it (Matt. 6:14–15). Considering that it is the one line in the Prayer that Jesus chose to reinforce with a kind of appendix, we cannot skip over it or wish it away. We have to face it head-on and deal with its implications, remembering that our own forgiveness is closely tied to our ability to come to terms with it.

How should we look at this? Perhaps the best way is to go back over the rest of the prayer and recall how it is constructed. As we have seen several times in the earlier sections, the Lord's Prayer maintains a delicate balance between the spiritual world (heaven) and the material world (earth). These two dimensions of reality are not equal or interchangeable, and there can be no doubt that the heavenly realm is superior and so must take priority in our thinking. But at the same time, the earthly side of things is never forgotten or devalued. It may be inferior in some sense, and it has problems that have to be put right in a way that heaven does not, but we must not forget that the whole purpose of Christ's coming was to meet the needs of earth by bringing the realities of the heavenly world to bear on its problems and to resolve them accordingly. If we think in this way, we shall realize that the first part of this line concentrates our minds on heaven, since we are praying to God and asking him to forgive us. The second part of it shifts the focus to earth, because now we are talking about the way we relate to our fellow human beings. If the general principle of the relationship between heaven and earth is applied here, we are entitled to say that the forgiveness God has given us in heaven is meant to be applied by us to our relationships with other human beings on earth.

Is this the right interpretation of this verse? Superficially, it looks as if we are expected to forgive others first and then God will forgive us accordingly. That cannot be right, though, because if it were true, it would turn our heavenly forgiveness into a work we would be able to achieve by forgiving others around us. It cannot be the case that we should forgive our fellow human beings merely in order to create a good impression with God, who is unlikely to be impressed by our efforts, however sincere they may be. If God does not want sacrifices offered directly to him, why should he be influenced by acts of forgiveness offered to other people, especially since many of these are bound to be fairly trivial in the overall scheme of things? Would God forgive me more if I forgave my son's murderer than if I forgave the man who wrecked my car, or the woman who accidentally stepped on my toe? Is there a scale of divine forgiveness calculated in direct relation to the forgiveness we show to others?

Clearly, this is an absurdity. God's forgiveness is absolute and eternal, because he is the absolute being. It cannot be calibrated according to the way in which we forgive others, which is always relative and contingent on circumstances. If we were dependent on this, we would never be sure whether God was forgiving us or not.

It makes much more sense to argue that God's forgiveness of us is the ground and motivation for our forgiveness of others and this ties in much better with what the Bible says elsewhere. If we interpret the verse that way, it sounds very much like something else Jesus said: 'You shall love the Lord your God with all your heart and with all your soul and with all your mind. This is the great and first commandment. And a second is like it: You shall love your neighbour as yourself' (Matt. 22:37–39). This is the principle at work here, although it is expressed in a slightly different way. We cannot love God without recognizing him for who he is. But we cannot recognize who he is without seeing that he is holy, and thus unable to tolerate our sinfulness. Therefore, we cannot love him without asking for his forgiveness, since there is no other way we can enter his presence. But having experienced the love of God for us, what can we do apart from seek to extend that love to others? And if there are those in the world who have offended us in some way, how can we extend God's love to them, other than by forgiving them? Forgiving others is certainly not the only way of showing God's love towards them, but it is one way, and a very important one. It is the key to reconciliation and the re-establishment of a functioning relationship, from which all our other duties will flow in due course. If we do not get over the first hurdle we shall not get any farther, and so the spirit of forgiveness plays a crucial role in our outreach to those around us.

Another way to look at the matter is this. When we have our minds attuned to heaven, it is as supplicants. We have sinned against God, but he has not sinned against us, and we are not entitled to his forgiveness. The only reason we can pray to him at all is that he has promised to forgive us and has made this possible through the death of his Son, who has paid the price for our sins. But when we turn to consider other people, the focus shifts. In the Lord's Prayer, we are not expected to ask God to forgive them in the same way he has forgiven us, though no doubt it would be perfectly proper for us to do so. On the contrary, we are expected to offer them our forgiveness, and what kind of gift would that be if it were not an extension of God's forgiveness towards us? Would other people really benefit from what we might be able to cobble together out of our own spiritual resources? Would our forgiveness towards them be tinged with a sense of guilt or obligation on our part, which would effectively cancel out any feeling of love? Do we want other people to think that we are forgiving them in a grudging spirit, or with an ulterior motive of some kind? Could we even call that forgiveness? We have to admit that our forgiveness of others would be suspect and worth very little if it were not underpinned by God's forgiveness. Those who have been forgiven much love much, and it is only from an abundance of that love that the forgiveness of our hearts can overflow into the hearts and lives of other people.

If this is the overall pattern of forgiveness – from God to us, from heaven to earth, from our hearts to the lives of other people – what are we to make of Jesus' warning that if we fail to forgive others, then God will not forgive us? Is this warning not proof that there is a sense in which God's behaviour towards us depends on our behaviour towards other people? Once again, we have to interpret this in the wider context of our relationship with God and his expectations of us within that relationship. The importance of forgiving others may be directly compared with the importance of loving our neighbours, and of that there can be no doubt whatsoever.

> If a brother or sister is poorly clothed and lacking in daily food, and one of you says to them, 'Go in peace, be warmed and filled,' without giving them the things needed for the body, what good is that? So also faith by itself, if it does not have works, is dead. (Jas 2:15–17)

Few things in the history of the Christian church are sadder than the opposition Martin Luther set up between the Pauline doctrine of justification by faith alone, to which he was rightly attached, and the epistle of James, which he regarded as lacking in spiritual authority because it says that faith without works is dead. Even today it is not unknown for preachers to insist on this distinction and to relegate James to secondary status because it appears to contradict the teaching of Paul. The tragedy is that this interpretation is based on a misunderstanding. James did not say that works were necessary for justification, as if God needed some evidence of our good intentions before giving us salvation. For James, works are not a cause of salvation but their consequence. Those who have faith are expected to demonstrate that they have it by the way they behave, and if they do not do so, their claim to have faith must be rejected. There is no such thing as a 'dead faith'; what James means by this expression is that such a person has no faith at all and never has had any.

Objectively speaking, it may seem that forgiving other people for the sins they have committed against us should be easier than asking God to forgive us. After all, God has no obligations towards us and there is no reason why he should listen to our pleas when the fault is entirely on our side. But other human beings are imperfect creatures just as we are and need forgiveness, either from us or from others, just as much as we do. Surely, it ought to be possible to recognize that by forgiving one another, we are helping one another out in good neighbourly fashion, and looked at in that way, there would not seem too much difficulty in it. One good turn deserves another, we might say, and realize that ultimately it is all in our own self-interest. Forgiving other people also involves matters that are only temporal and relative, and must therefore be far less serious than sins against God. Time the great healer does not operate in heaven, where there is no time, but we may assume that on earth the passage of the years will dull the memory and put everything in a different perspective. For example, many people still find it hard to forgive the Germans for the bombings of the Second World War, but who now blames the Romans for having invaded Britain nearly two thousand years ago, or the Normans for what happened in 1066? Probably only the British could have made Waterloo the London terminal for the Eurostar train service from Paris, but not even the touchiest Frenchman has ever suggested that this should be

a *casus belli*.[6] Time has moved on, ancient wounds have healed and
the few people who cannot 'forgive and forget' are left stranded as
the tide of history sweeps past them and carries their sacred
causes into oblivion.

What is true of nations is surely also true on the much reduced
scale of our own individual lives, but although this is often the
case, we all know that forgiving other people can be much harder
than asking God to forgive us. Perhaps it is because we feel that
God does not really suffer when we offend him. We think he is
much too big to be seriously affected by anything we might do and
that consequently it is easy for him to brush it off. But when other
people offend us, it is not so easy for us to regard the matter as
equally insignificant. We are not as detached from that sort of
thing as we imagine God to be; we cannot just turn away from
someone who may have done us real harm and pretend that it
does not matter. Then too, we do not stand in the same kind of
relationship to other people as we do to God. We are not their cre-
ators, for a start, and so there is no a priori reason why we should
love them as beings whom we have made. We feel no unbreakable
bond tying us to them and may not have anything to do with them
apart from the offence they have caused. It is always much easier
to deal harshly with those whom we neither know nor care about,
and in this sense we can say that we stand in a different relationship to most other people than God does.

In dealing with this issue, the first thing we have to do is accept
the fact that other people sin against us, and that we sin against
them too, whether we want to do so or not. The fall of the human
race has this catastrophic effect. It not only sets us against God,
but against each other as well. It would be nice to think that the
church is the happy fellowship of the redeemed who all get along
beautifully together, but the reality is often very different. Christian
communities are frequently divided by internal factions, by leaders
who are out to satisfy their own pride and not to serve the church,

---

6. From its opening in 1994 until 2007, the main London terminal for the
   Eurostar was Waterloo. Since 14 November 2007 it has moved to St
   Pancras, though for practical reasons, and not to keep the French happy!

by members who refuse to pull their weight or act as good team
players. Anyone involved in church life will be only too familiar
with this sort of thing from bitter experience. There is no sense in
pretending otherwise. I once lived and worked in a community
that refused to accept the reality of human sinfulness and the
result was a complete disaster. Pretending that there was a close
fellowship between the members when in fact there was none at all
merely exacerbated the many problems that needed to be solved,
and in the end the whole community broke up in a most ungodly
way. The saddest part of this whole sorry business was that
nobody asked for forgiveness, because nobody believed they had
done anything wrong. They almost all believed that the trouble
had come from somewhere else. Either Satan had decided to step
in and cause problems (a favourite explanation in some circles) or
there had been a Judas in the ranks who was hiding his true
colours. To face up to the simple fact that sinful people will create
sinful communities, and to accept that there will be a constant
need for everyone involved to repent and ask for forgiveness is not
to despair of the grace of God, but to recognize that we need to
do this because of the fundamental brokenness of human life that
will not be put right until the coming of the new heaven and the
new earth at the end of time (Rev. 21:1–2).

Of course, here as everywhere, we must be aware of the subtle
corruptions that can creep in and distort the human need for
repentance and forgiveness. There are some people who go out of
their way to seek forgiveness from other people, not because they
genuinely feel they need it but as a way of applying spiritual pressure or of demonstrating spiritual superiority over them. They will
approach others out of the blue and inform them that they have
been offended by something or other that that particular person
has done, knowingly or otherwise. They will then add that they
have found it in their hearts to forgive the wrong done to them,
when in fact they were never offended at all and are simply using
this form of mock-humility as a way of declaring their spiritual
authority over others. The poor person who has allegedly
caused the offence may be totally mystified by this and even be
deeply remorseful for something he or she has not actually done,
thus allowing the one who claims to have been offended to gain an

unhealthy spiritual ascendancy as the 'offender' struggles to put matters right.

That kind of behaviour is quite wrong, of course. Jesus does not say that we should go around seeking forgiveness from other people but that we should forgive them in our hearts. Whether we should approach them personally is not easy to determine in the abstract. If it is clear I have offended someone and that person knows it, then the answer is probably yes, we should approach the offended party. But what if I think that I have offended another person but there is no sign that person has any idea of it? You may wonder how that is possible, but it has actually happened to me and so I know that it is. A student of mine once came up to me and apologized for having said bad things about me behind my back. I had no idea that he had done so and scarcely knew what to say to him. In the end I said that whatever he imagined about me was not nearly as bad as the truth, which was mercifully hidden from his eyes. I was not offended, but I was left puzzled. Inevitably, there followed a period of some awkwardness in our relationship because I was afraid that whatever I said or did would be interpreted by him as evidence of whether I had really forgiven him or not. In particular, it occurred to me quite quickly that if I were to give him a bad mark on his course work, he might easily have interpreted that as a sign that I had not forgiven him and was getting my revenge in the nastiest way I could. It was a difficult period to negotiate, though I am glad to say we succeeded in the end and things seem to have reverted to normal fairly quickly. Even so, I think I would probably have been better off if he had said nothing to me at all, since I was, and presumably would have remained, completely oblivious to the whole thing!

There is also the problem of what to do when the spirit of forgiveness is on one side only. This often happens, especially in close relationships that break up, and it requires a particular kind of sensitivity if we are to deal with it properly. I remember very well one occasion when a close friend of mine fell out with some of the colleagues he worked with. There was a great deal of bitterness on all sides and eventually he was forced to leave his company because the atmosphere had degenerated to the point where mutual trust and co-operation had completely vanished. He was made the scapegoat for this and was forced to resign his job, although he was by no means chiefly responsible for what had happened, and far guiltier people escaped unscathed. People kept urging my friend to forgive his colleagues for what they had done to him and not to bear a grudge against them, even though both he and they knew perfectly well that the fault lay on all sides and that he had been unfairly treated. It was hard for him to accept this at first, but in the end he got to that point, only to discover that his former colleagues had not. As far as they were concerned, they had been entirely in the right, had no need to ask this man for his forgiveness, had no intention of asking him back to work and thought that his offer of forgiveness and reconciliation was presumptuous and insincere. It was all too clear that they had no sense of their own responsibility, and that there would not have been the slightest degree of reciprocity towards his overtures. What do you do in a situation like that?

The answer must be that it is possible to forgive others without achieving reconciliation with them. In God's dealings with us the two go together, but God is perfect and it would be impossible for his forgiveness not to be accompanied by reconciliation. Unfortunately, human beings are not perfect, and in our relationships with one another this kind of dissonance is sometimes inevitable. It is particularly poignant when a marriage relationship breaks down and after a time one of the parties seeks reconciliation, only to discover that the other has lost interest. In such a situation, forgiveness can only be an attitude of heart and mind waiting for an opportunity to manifest itself if the occasion should arise, but not demanding that it should before the forgiveness can become a reality. It may be that the only outward manifestation of a forgiving attitude will be a refusal to seek revenge, either by doing something to hurt the other person or by saying things that would make it clear we do not think much of them or of their behaviour. Silence and inactivity may be the best course to follow, because even if it does little good it will not make the situation any worse. This is a sign of forgiveness but it is not reconciliation, which can take place only if the other party agrees to it. We have no control over this and it may not be possible for other reasons. For example, the other party may have died, putting

closure to the relationship for the time being. An estranged spouse
may easily have gone off with someone else and remarried, making
a restoration of the earlier relationship a practical impossibility.
The people concerned may have lost contact with each other and
have no way of getting in touch. Even if they do, others may not
be interested in raking over the past and feel that it is best simply
to let bygones be bygones. Trying to force ourselves on to people
like that will not work and may even be counterproductive, especially if they start wondering what our motives might be.

For reconciliation to occur it must be desired by both parties. If
they are Christians, this ought to be possible, because of our
mutual desire to serve God. Sometimes it is, and we must praise
him for that when it happens. But sometimes it is not, and there is
nothing we can do about it. This is particularly true when the
problem is not between individuals but between communities.
Anyone who has lived through a church split knows how hard it
can be to seek reconciliation afterwards. The reasons for such
splits are many and varied, and usually there is right and wrong on
both sides, making it very difficult to make a clear choice for one
or the other. If the split involves wider denominational politics, it
becomes even more difficult to resolve, since each side in the
dispute is to some extent playing proxy for other people or ideas
that may be far removed from local circumstances. Something of
this kind is currently happening in many Protestant churches,
where the central administrative body has been taken over by one
particular group (usually a liberal extreme) that is trying to impose
its new ideas on the denomination as a whole. Individual congregations may then be divided between those who think it right to
secede from the denomination and those who do not. It may even
be the case that both sides in the dispute disagree with the policy
being laid down at the centre; what they are arguing about is not
the problem itself, but only the best way of dealing with it! The
possible complications and permutations are endless, but the bitterness that disputes create comes out regardless and remains to
sour the atmosphere long after the problem that caused it has disappeared. How do we forgive this, when it may well be that our
church owes its very existence to such a split? How do we seek reconciliation, especially after generations have passed, when it may

look like repudiating the witness of our founders? This problem is not confined to Protestants. One of the biggest difficulties preventing the reunion of the Chalcedonian and non-Chalcedonian churches of the East is that each has a roll call of its saints and martyrs, many of whom suffered and died at the hands of the other side. Would reunion mean denying the witness of these martyrs after more than fifteen centuries? That may be an extreme case, but it serves to remind us that church splits can have lasting consequences, and the inability to forgive and forget may play a major part in sustaining them long after the original cause of the dispute has been forgotten or resolved.

In conclusion, we can only say that forgiving others is not easy. The words 'As we forgive those who trespass against us' remain a challenging benchmark we shall never find easy or painless. May God forgive us for our failures in this respect and teach us how we can do battle with ourselves to make this command of his a reality in our lives, so that we may truly be able to say that we can forgive others as we have been forgiven by God, and that by forgiving, we can bring hope and reconciliation to a dark and dangerous world.

5. LEAD US NOT INTO TEMPTATION, BUT DELIVER US FROM EVIL

Spiritual warfare

At first sight, the last sentence in the Lord's Prayer comes across as fairly negative, because it concentrates on the related, though by no means identical, themes of temptation and evil. But when we examine it more closely, we see that in fact this petition is a compendium of the Christian life, which is a spiritual struggle between the believer, who is inspired and fortified by the indwelling presence of God's Holy Spirit, and the power of Satan, the prince of this world and our former ruler, who does not sit idly by as his subjects are taken from him and made citizens of the kingdom of heaven.

If we look back on the Lord's Prayer as a whole, we can see that each sentence of it takes us one step further into the mystery of God and our salvation. It starts with 'Our Father', the words with which Jesus taught us to address the first person of the Trinity, whose great work is to represent the sovereign otherness of God to us in his holy name. Then it moves on to the incarnation of Christ, the coming of the king and his kingdom, and the work he did, in bringing the will of God to reign on earth as it does in heaven. From there the prayer goes on to speak of how the fruits of that finished work are applied in our lives, by the giving of daily bread, both physical and spiritual, and by the forgiveness of sins. Now we come to the crowning glory – the work of the Holy Spirit, who teaches us to live the new life we have in Christ. The different petitions, which seem to be disjointed and unconnected when we first look at them, reveal themselves to be profoundly linked at the theological level. Each line of the Lord's Prayer teaches us something more about our relationship with God and how this works out in our experience. With this last sentence we come to the most challenging theme of all, which touches every aspect of our lives. Furthermore, it is an area where we often fail, but where failure is frequently not acknowledged, and therefore not overcome. The more we study it, the more we shall find ourselves persuaded of the need to adopt a kind of spiritual fitness programme, which will sanctify us and bring us closer to the heavenly destiny that the Father has foreordained and that his Son has gone to prepare for us.

That the Christian life is a spiritual warfare is a common New Testament theme that has had many echoes down through the centuries. The greatest writer on the subject in English, John Bunyan, expressed it well when he wrote these famous lines:

> Who so beset him round
>   With dismal stories,
> Do but themselves confound;
>   His strength the more is.
> No lion can him fright,
> He'll with a giant fight,
> But he will have a right
>   To be a pilgrim.

Bunyan's words have resonated in the lives of many, but although we still sing them today, their deeper message often seems to have fallen silent in the modern church. Not everywhere, of course, and not with everyone, but more so perhaps than at any time since he wrote them. Instead of the picture of the pilgrim fighting with giants on his way to the Celestial City, the modern narrative of the Christian journey often comes across somewhat differently. Today we usually hear people start with their pre-conversion life of sin, which may be told in excruciating detail, ostensibly in order to exalt the grace of God but more probably in order to entertain the audience with tales of wickedness and vice that are usually much more interesting than mere virtue. Then, at a point in the story where it scarcely seems that things could get any worse, God steps in and the sinner experiences a sudden turnaround. The man or woman who had been lost in sin is born again, finds a good church, creates the perfect family and goes off to live happily ever after. The subtext of this narrative is that when you accept Jesus, everything will work out fine and you will never have any more problems. Since this is the message the modern church wants to convey in order to attract new members, conversion stories of this kind are encouraged and promoted. Very seldom are we likely to hear anything less attractive or less encouraging, at least not from the pulpit. Let us be honest and admit that there are people with such success stories, and that there have been some amazing conversions from the most unlikely starting points, for which we must be grateful to God. The Christian life is indeed a wonderful new beginning and we must always remember to emphasize that fact in our preaching and teaching. No-one has fallen so far from the grace of God that he or she cannot be rescued and restored, and we must never fail to hold out the promise of this to those in need.

Having said that, I think we must also admit that such people are relatively rare and that most Christians have led fairly ordinary lives before their conversion. Men and women come to Christ in any number of different ways but most of them are pretty undramatic. I must confess that I have often been slightly embarrassed to give a testimony of how I came to faith because I had never done anything dramatically wrong beforehand, and, by Hollywood standards, my conversion was exceedingly dull and boring. That does not make it less real, and it has always been very important to me personally, but you would not want to read the book if one should ever appear on the subject for the simple reason that you would fall asleep after the first five pages! It is difficult for me to say what difference my conversion made to my life in economic or social terms. I came from a middle-class family and had a typically middle-class upbringing with no surprises or complications. My parents were happily married, we had a good family life and there was never the slightest hint of alcoholism, indebtedness or infidelity in anyone I grew up with. It was a safe environment, full of nice people who were honest, hard-working and dependable, for which I shall be eternally grateful. I could and did become a Christian with little or no outward change of appearance or lifestyle and I went on to achieve the kinds of goals in life that anyone of my background might aspire to, whether a believer or not. There is very little about the outward course of my life that I can honestly say was specifically Christian. To all intents and purposes I was perfectly normal, accepted by my peers, encouraged by my family and given a good start in life. At the same time, I have no doubt whatsoever that during my teenage years I came to a living faith in Christ, who has stayed close to me and remained central to my life more than a generation later, and that in the longer term it has made all the difference to the way I have lived my life. What might seem unremarkable in social terms has turned out to be revolutionary and life-changing in spiritual ones, even if there has been little or no outward upheaval to accompany it.

In statistical terms, this kind of trajectory is undoubtedly far more common than the dramatic conversion from a life of debauchery, even though the latter attracts more attention. People like me, who experience what we might call ordinary, run-of-the mill conversions, may not have much of a story to tell about their previous life, but this serves only to highlight something more important, which the typical modern conversion narrative does not mention. To put it bluntly, this is that the Christian's real troubles begin at conversion; they do not end there. That was certainly true in my case. My parents could not accept that I would adopt such unscientific notions as belief in the bodily resurrection of Jesus. They became more critical of my teenage behaviour than they had been before, because as a Christian I was supposed to be perfect and quite clearly was not. Ironically, even though they did not accept my beliefs, they still expected my behaviour to improve dramatically because of them, and did not hesitate to judge me by a standard of which I was then only partially aware. My choice of career was another bone of contention. Ever since Martin Luther objected to the sale of indulgences, a career in the church has not been especially lucrative – quite the reverse in fact – and my father had not brought me up in order that I should live in relative poverty for the rest of my life. Thus it was that one way or another, my undramatic conversion brought about a gradual and deepening alienation from my family and former friends. Eventually, my parents came to accept that my Christian friends were not members of some secret cult and did not do strange things in the middle of the night, but that took a while to sink in and the scars left by those years have never fully healed. Even now when I go to visit my family I still have to insist on finding time to go to church, since it is not in their calendar and they have often planned to do other things then that they want to include me in. None of this compares to being thrown to the lions in the Coliseum, of course, but it is a form of struggle many people identify with and can sometimes be very painful, because it affects the closest relationships we have with other people on earth.

Later in life, problems of this kind can multiply. For example, a Christian employee may discover that he or she cannot conscientiously accept the policies of his company. It is one thing for the chief executive officer to act like a Christian when there is nobody to tell him or her to do otherwise, but it is not so easy for those lower down the totem pole. Recently there was the well-publicized case of Nadia Edeewa, a check-in clerk at British Airways who insisted on wearing a cross around her neck as a sign of her Christian faith, even though it supposedly went against the company's policy on the wearing of 'jewellery'. She pointed out that Muslim women could wear the hijab and others could wear equally distinctive dress on religious grounds, but that as a Christian she was being discriminated against. The obtuse reaction of British Airways, which stuck to its 'rule' until it was forced to back down in the face of mounting opposition from Members of Parliament and even bishops, gave credence to the claim that she had indeed been singled out, and other Christians could tell a similar story.

The problem seems to be that in a nominally Christian country, people who follow minority religions stand out and are protected precisely because of that, whereas Christians are not supposed to be any different from the nominal majority. When they stand out because of their beliefs, that majority is often puzzled. This is because, on the one hand, it does not share these convictions, but, on the other hand, it does not think of itself as being non-Christian either. As a result, Christians can find it almost as hard to stand up for their faith in a nominally Christian country as they would in a place where they are a recognized cultural minority. Either way, it can be costly to be a believer, and Christians must be prepared for incomprehension at home even more than for hostility abroad.

Christians may also have to make hard choices about marriage, which can be very costly. It is all too easy to fall in love with an unsuitable person. The heartache caused by a broken romance is exceeded only by the pain caused by a mixed or broken marriage, which may easily be the result when people go ahead regardless of the consequences. Here it must be said that the church is often more to blame than is publicly acknowledged. There is often a lot of pressure put on single people to marry if they can, and the desire for a spouse can easily dull the judgment of those looking for one. Once the choice is made, the church may be so committed to marital success, which many people think is meant to come almost automatically to the true believer, that it is ill prepared to deal with the many breakdowns that occur. How many bitter people are there in our midst, who feel that they have been let down by God and that there is no place for them in the church because they have failed to live up to its expectations in the sphere of marriage?

Other Christians may have to face lingering illness, for which there is no ready cure. Jesus performed miracles of physical healing and said to the disciples of John the Baptist, when they came to enquire about him, 'Go and tell John what you hear and see: the blind receive their sight and the lame walk, lepers are cleansed and the deaf hear, and the dead are raised up' (Matt. 11:4–5). It is an inspiring message, but it may be cold comfort to those who are suffering from such disabilities and have not experienced a miraculous healing. Why not? Does Jesus show partiality? Has he lost his power to heal? The continuing appeal of miracle-workers and faith healers can only be explained by this unfulfilled desire on the part of so many who turn to Jesus for a cure but do not find one. It is all very well for those who are not suffering to point out that the signs Jesus did had a special prophetic significance that cannot be replicated today, and to add that the healing people so desperately want will be given to them in heaven, but how many of us would voluntarily submit to such disabilities as part of our spiritual struggle in this life? For many Christians there is no choice, and we who are fortunate enough to have been spared such agonies must take special care to be sympathetic to those who bear this kind of burden and to support them in every way we can.

No-one can predict what particular form his or her own spiritual struggle will take, but every Christian must face the fact that we are called to take up our cross and follow Jesus. It is not for us to complain if the particular battle we are asked to fight is not to our taste. The precise details will be different for different people – Peter was told he would die a martyr's death, but was not to object if John were spared – because God deals with each of us differently (John 21:21–22). The only thing we can be sure of is that we shall be touched by spiritual warfare one way or another, because, whether we like it or not, each of us is a soldier in the Lord's army. It is particularly important for evangelical Christians to understand this and to remember that we are the enemy's prime targets. The objective reason for this is clear enough – because we are believers who proclaim our faith openly and challenge others to take it for themselves or leave it, we are highly unpopular people. Church leaders who would not dream of saying anything that might be remotely offensive to someone of another religion, or to social minorities like homosexuals or drug addicts, think nothing of pilloring evangelicals in the most derogatory terms. Often they do not even bother to check their facts or consider whether their remarks are fair or not. Because it is so patently obvious to them that evangelicals are obnoxious, they think they can say anything they like and get away with it, like the dean of an English cathedral who saw nothing wrong in comparing them to the Taliban fighters in Afghanistan, a group of fanatics whom he thought were equally objectionable and therefore indistinguishable from evangelical Christians!

Those who are used to the rough and tumble of politics take things like this in their stride, but there are many people who live more sheltered lives or who have not been Christians long enough to have developed a thick skin in the face of such jibes. It can be very hurtful to be unjustly attacked in that way, and we must never underestimate the psychological damage that can be done to tender souls. How many people are there in high office today, even in the church, who have learned to trim their Christian convictions to suit the prevailing winds of political correctness, because they cannot bear the pain that would be caused if they stood out from the crowd and took a stand? Not long ago the Bishop of Chester was threatened with possible prosecution by the local chief of police because he dared to suggest that some homosexuals might be cured of their disorder. He had offended a powerful lobby, even if what he said was true, and was told that if he did so again he might face prosecution. What should the poor man have done in such a situation? To make matters even worse, he was not publicly supported by his fellow bishops, some of whom were undoubtedly more sympathetic to the chief of police than they were to him. It is one thing to have to suffer persecution from the outside world, but when it comes from within the church, as it often does, it is much harder to take.

The only comfort in such a situation is to remember that Jesus was persecuted most relentlessly by those who held the highest positions in the Jewish community of his day. The Romans were not sympathetic to his cause but would never have crucified him if the Jews had not insisted on it. It is much the same today. Unbelievers, particularly those in the media, take the occasional swing at evangelicals, and if they have done a bit of homework can appear to be reasonably well informed in their criticisms. One such attack appeared a few years ago in a book with the title *A Church at War*.[1] This was meant to be an exposé of the conflict within the Anglican Communion, and particularly within the Church of England, which had arisen in the wake of the consecration of a practising homosexual as bishop of New Hampshire in the USA. As far as the author was concerned, the villains of the

---

1. S. A. Bates, *A Church at War: Anglicans and Homosexuality* (London: Taurus, 2004). Mr Bates is religion correspondent for the *Guardian* newspaper.

piece were the religious conservatives, who rapidly turned out to be almost exclusively evangelicals. As he saw it, these dreadful people were forming alliances with churches in the developing world, withholding funds from their own churches in order to bribe poorer ones overseas into supporting them in their fight against 'inclusivity' and 'justice' and generally being as obnoxious as possible. Being a journalist himself, he had no qualms about naming names, and a glance through the index reads like a who's who of the evangelical world.

It was a bad book and many people were appalled by its level of reporting and almost vicious bias. Some felt hurt at having been so unfairly treated, but given the nature of the attack, to be included among the ranks of the condemned was not a disgrace but an honour. The only people who needed to feel ashamed were prominent evangelicals who had *not* been mentioned, because the inevitable question must be asked of them – why were they not singled out as well? Had they been too afraid to stand up and be counted? Keeping your head below the parapet and having nice things said about you by all and sundry is not a good recommendation for those who follow the man accused of eating and drinking on the Sabbath, of associating with sinners and of teaching his followers to do likewise on the ground that the inward disposition of the heart is more important than conformity to outward rituals. As Christians we should never go looking for persecution, but if it comes our way we must not run away from it and hide either. Peter did this on the night Jesus was betrayed and the memory of that dreadful moment of weakness has been preserved for posterity in the Gospels (Matt. 26:69–75). Fortunately, that was not the end for him, and he was reconciled to Jesus after the resurrection, but his actions in Pilate's courtyard are a reminder to us that if the chief of the apostles could behave like that, then none of us is safe. Put us in the wrong place at the wrong time and we too might easily find ourselves denying our Lord, only to regret it bitterly once the moment has passed.

Times are hard for those who stand up for the truth. It was always so and it will not change until our Lord returns and gives the ungodly the fruits of his judgment. We ought therefore to examine what we must do to prepare ourselves for battle. We cannot say what part of the struggle we shall be called upon to engage in, but there will be no deferral for the faithful Christian. Wherever it is and however it appears, the spiritual fight is one we shall be called upon to wage. It will be tough going, because the devil knows our weaknesses and is quick to aim his shafts at them. To defeat him we must put on the whole armour of God (Eph. 6:11), and to that we now turn our attention.

Lead us not into temptation

'Know your enemy' is a maxim any military strategist will put near the top of his list of priorities, if not at the top itself. Those who study the history of warfare know only too well that armies are often prepared to fight the last war, but are seldom able to deal adequately with the conflict in front of them. The Maginot Line in France stands as a classic monument to this tendency, as do the defences of Singapore. Today we have weapons of mass destruction that can wipe out whole cities in an instant, but our armies are lost when it comes to detecting terrorist cells that hide out among perfectly ordinary people in leafy suburbia. The enemy has changed his tactics and we scarcely know what to do about it. In 1945, it was widely believed that the invention of atomic weapons would make future wars impossible, and that the fear which had gripped people for six years would become a distant memory. Yet today, well within the lifetime of many who lived through those years, we panic at the sight of a bag left unattended on a railway station platform. Our lives have been turned upside down by security measures that not only restrict our movements but sometimes even threaten our fundamental liberties. The danger of being caught up in war, which in the 1940s was generally restricted to people who found themselves in recognized combat zones, has now become almost universal and every one of us lives in at least low-level fear of possible attack.

In spiritual matters the problem is much the same. In the early years of the Christian church, there were people who tried to escape persecution by running away into the desert. They hid in caves, which saved them from the Romans, but soon discovered that the desert was a place of spiritual warfare more challenging than anything the state had to offer. Released from the constraints of ordinary society, these men were free to do battle with the devil, and their writings testify to struggles of which lesser mortals are scarcely aware. Even if we think that the heat of the noonday sun deranged some of them and distorted their thinking, so that they began to see Satan under every bush, as it were, there is still enough to remind us of the extraordinary power of the enemy we face.

Later, after persecution ceased, Christians found that they had to do battle for their faith, not against pagan enemies who did not understand anything about them, but against heretics from within the church who did their best to divert it from the pure message of the gospel – sometimes with the emperor's help. The truth is that we can defeat our enemy in one way only to discover that he has found a new tactic more subtle and terrifying than the last one. No Christians are in bigger trouble than those who have just won a victory in their struggles and think they can relax because the danger is now past. In reality, they are more vulnerable than ever. Pastors soon learn that the most difficult times in their lives often come immediately after they have preached their heart out in a well-crafted and effective sermon. They have given their all, emptying themselves for the sake of the gospel, and Satan is on hand to take advantage of their exhaustion. The smallest touch of pride at apparent success and he has them hooked; their downfall is only moments away and indeed has already begun in spiritual terms. The slightest relaxation of our guard is enough for the enemy to pounce. Fortunately, most of the time, God is gracious to us and we are rescued from our folly in the nick of time. But every once in a while we hear of a successful pastor somewhere, or of a well-known evangelist, who was not so protected and who fell into sin and disgrace as a result. Experienced Christian ministers are not surprised by such things, because they know only too well that there, but for the grace of God, goes any of us. This is the enemy we are up against. It is this battle that we are forced to fight in our own lives as much as in the lives of those whom we are called to serve.

The beginning of all the trouble is temptation. This is made clear in the opening chapters of Genesis. Adam and Eve did not get up one day and decide to disobey God just to see what would happen to them. They were not looking for something to relieve the boredom of living in a perfect environment. Their fall did not start with them but with Satan, who came to them and offered them something that appeared to be highly desirable. Taking the form of a serpent, Satan told them that he knew how they could become like God. What a wonderful thing, you might think. What could possibly be wrong about becoming more like God? Is this not what we proclaim from our pulpits every Sunday? Is it not what God himself tells us, when he says, 'You shall be holy, for I am holy' (Lev. 20:7; 1 Pet. 1:16)? Surely, Satan was doing Adam and Eve a service by pointing out to them how they could achieve the most desirable goal of all! Note too, that the key to reaching that goal was not something beyond their capacities. They were not expected to climb up to heaven, which would have been impossible, nor were they asked to devote hours of time to spiritual exercises on earth, which might have ended up discouraging them. On the contrary, it was all so simple. All they had to do was to eat the fruit of the tree that was right there in front of their eyes, and the miracle would be achieved – they would become like God!

Furthermore, what Satan had promised them was true enough as far as it went. Like a good salesman who never actually lies to you, he told them the truth – up to a point. He obviously had a way with words, because even though they knew that God had told them otherwise, they ate the fruit and became more like God, something that even God himself acknowledged (Gen. 3:22). It had worked! The snag of course, is that Satan had told them only part of the story. He had neglected to point out that by following his advice, Adam and Eve would be signing away their lives to him without realizing it. We know what his tactics were like because every once in a while some television reporter does an exposé of this kind of thing. People who have given money to a fraudster on a promise of instant wealth discover that they have to keep contributing ever larger sums for the results to be seen, and before they know it they have handed over everything they have got and received nothing more for it than a bucketful of empty promises. This is what happened to Adam and Eve. You can almost hear them crying into the camera, 'We thought we were going to have the perfect retirement in the garden and now we have ended up with nothing!'

The beauty of temptation is that it seems to promise so much in return for something that looks easy and readily achievable. Temptation gives us that incredible feeling of empowerment by telling us that if we give in to it we shall gain control of our destiny, do what we want and escape our tiresome obligations. When President Bill Clinton was asked how he could possibly have fallen for the likes of Monica Lewinsky and jeopardized both his career and his marriage, he was honest enough to admit that he did it because as the most powerful man in the world, he could do almost anything he wanted to. He thought he would get away with it, and the prospect of public humiliation never seems to have crossed his mind. The rest of us live on a humbler plane, but the mechanics of temptation are still the same. Even when it comes to us, it still has that magic ability to seem attractive, advantageous and achievable all at once. If it strikes us at a moment when we are particularly vulnerable, there is every chance that we shall fall just as Adam and Eve fell. The worst thing we can do is to imagine that we have some automatic protection against temptation, that it will never happen to us, that we can do whatever we want to do because, as children of God, nobody can touch us. Not for nothing does the Bible warn us that

Pride goes before destruction,
and a haughty spirit before a fall.
(Prov. 16:18)

Let us take another example to show how temptation can work in the life of the church, and not just in the lives of individual believers. We live in a time of declining church attendance and influence, when even its workers may be under serious threat of redundancy. In such a situation, we can easily be persuaded that the answer must be church growth, and specialists in this subject are on hand to help us achieve it. No-one will dispute that winning souls for the kingdom of God is a good idea, so church growth is on the side of the angels to start with. Indeed, church decline can easily be presented as a form of rebellion and unbelief, because if we were being faithful witnesses it would not have happened in the first place! There is so much self-evident truth in these propositions

that it is hard to see what could possibly be wrong with a programme designed to promote the growth of a church. In one
sense, of course, there is not. I can certainly agree with the church-
growth experts that God increases his blessings to those who are
faithful, and that in many cases this will result in thriving and
growing congregations, for which we must be duly grateful. The
hesitations I have are not with the goals but with something else.
As with Adam and Eve's becoming like God, it is not the end that
is the problem, but the means used to get there.

If we preach the Word without fear or favour, if we declare the
whole counsel of God to people whether they like it or not, if we
are prepared to cause offence for the sake of the gospel, then yes,
we may expect that God will bless us and reward us accordingly.
The snag is that all too often church-growth experts take their cue
not from the Bible but from the world of advertising. As they see
it, the product we offer has to appeal to the target audience, and if
it does not, then it must be changed until it does. The effects of
this approach can be very subtle. For example, we may be told that
preaching about sin and damnation is a turn-off to many people,
who are supposedly looking to the church for love and acceptance.
Harsh words about adultery or homosexuality are only going to
put people off, so it is better if we do not talk about them. Failure
and incompetence are further negatives, so we must not mention
the fact that we have all sinned against God in a way that we can
do nothing to redeem, and that our lives are a complete failure as a
result. Instead of discussing such negative things, we should talk
about the love of God that reaches out to embrace everyone,
whoever they are and whatever they may have done. People must
be made to feel welcome in the church, and that there is a place for
them there, that no-one will point a finger of judgment at them
that might turn them away.

The problem is not that any of this is untrue, but that it tells us
only half the story. As with Satan in the Garden of Eden, the
message itself is not false but it has so many holes in it that it
cannot be trusted as it stands. For example, it is quite true to say
that God reaches out to us where we are and accepts us into his
family, but his purpose in doing this is to change us so we can
become what he wants us to be. This change is radical, so radical

that the Bible calls it being 'born again'. God knows that we cannot do it on our own; we cannot even go to him with the operation half-started and ask him to sort out the rest. He has to start from the beginning and do the work himself – amateur assistance from us is not required, indeed it would be positively harmful. So in that sense, it is quite true to say that God takes us as we are – he has to.

But to say this and then leave the impression (if only by what is left out) that the condition we are in is quite all right, that we do not have to change in any significant way and that God will happily vindicate our current lifestyle, opinions and concerns if only we surrender ourselves to him, is to betray the message of the gospel. The sad result is that when we look around at our churches, we find that often they are full of people who think and behave in exactly the same way as the world around them. Even on a matter like marriage, where we might have reason to believe that church members would set a higher standard than others, statistics reveal (as mentioned earlier) that there is no appreciable difference in the divorce rate between those who attend Christian worship and those who do not. How can this be? The only answer is that the church has been filled by people who have not counted the cost of becoming a Christian, who have not realized that we are called to a different way of life the world does not know, who cannot understand what we are about and who will oppose us if they are confronted by what we stand for.

God's love is not to be confused with tolerance, and this is another way in which so many of us are tempted and go wrong. Instead of holding to high standards that drive us to repentance when we fail to meet them, we prefer to lower the barriers of acceptance. This is a widespread trend nowadays, and there are many parallels with it in everyday life. Anyone involved in education will know this from personal experience. Failure at school is thought to have such negative consequences on a child's psyche that everything must be done to prevent it from happening. If there are rules and standards that get in the way of this, then they must be bent in order to accommodate this overriding necessity. A student's inability to string two sentences together may be excused as the sad consequence of social deprivation or of having been taught according to an antiquated approach to learning. The 'differently gifted', as some of these people are occasionally referred to, are awarded the same certificate as everyone else, because to do otherwise would be to discriminate against the 'academically challenged'. When all else fails, there is usually a drunken father, a mother who was on drugs during her pregnancy or a bad part of town that can be dragged in to explain away what most people think of as laziness or as deviant forms of self-expression.

The cumulative result of this approach has been a steady dumbing down of our culture that is now so serious that in a society which boasts 100% literacy, the publishing industry faces real challenges and seems only to survive by printing vast quantities of picture books. This kind of thing would have shocked an earlier generation, but now the process of simplifying everything is routine, even in universities. In such an atmosphere, it is hardly surprising that we find a similar phenomenon in the church. People are accepted rather than challenged, affirmed rather than rebuked, and promoted rather than corrected, all because we are afraid that otherwise we shall lose them. The result is that we have a church where anything goes, where there is no discipline, and where ignorant and immoral people can become leaders simply because we are out to embrace all humanity. It is an absurd situation, but this is where temptation has taken us – the temptation to grow at all costs, whether the means we choose to do so are pleasing to God or not. The saddest thing of all, of course, is that despite all our efforts and the claims made for this or that technique to fill our churches, overall attendance continues to drop and the traditionally Christian world turns its back on the faith even more as the years go by.

Temptation and sin

Temptation is subtle and is a marvellous tool of the devil, but we must insist that in itself it is not sin. Many people think that it is, and worry because they imagine that as Christians they should be free from such things. There can be nothing more disheartening than to find people who have been defeated even before the battle has begun because they have mistaken the devil's opening attacks for his final victory over them. In these circumstances we need to remember that the apostle Paul tells us we shall never be tempted to a degree we cannot bear, even though we shall never be free of it altogether (1 Cor. 10:13). God does not tempt anyone himself (Jas 1:13); all temptation comes from the devil or from one of his agents. When we pray not to be led into it, we are not praying that we should escape it completely, but that when it comes we should not succumb to it. As we have already had occasion to observe, the psychology of temptation is very subtle. It looks good to start off with, and if we have any doubts about it, we are liable to suppress them by saying things like 'Once won't do us any harm' or 'Nobody will ever find out'. When we do this, we are being led into temptation; that is to say, we are being persuaded to give in to it. The fact that we often do this ourselves, without any prompting from the devil, shows just how much we need to pray this prayer. By asking God not to lead us into temptation, we are asking him to protect us against ourselves as much as against anyone else. Without this kind of self-control we shall get nowhere. John Milton said of Oliver Cromwell that he had fought many battles, but that his greatest battle of all was the one he fought against himself. What was true of Cromwell is true of us all – we are ultimately our own worst enemy. In the final analysis, not to be led into temptation is to be protected against ourselves, a tall order that makes the prayer all the more necessary.

We know that temptation is not the same thing as sin, because Jesus was tempted, although he was without sin. He resisted the temptations that came to him and defeated them, but this was not because he was immune to them or because they were not real. Indeed, one of the most interesting things about the temptations of Jesus recorded in Matthew 4 is that in their own way, they are a witness to the fact that he was God. You and I would never be tempted to turn stones into bread for the simple reason that it is beyond our ability to do so, but Jesus was tempted in that way, because he was God and could do what he liked with the created order. Satan evidently thought that after forty days of self-imposed starvation in the wilderness, Jesus might be persuaded to satisfy his earthly body by working a miracle. Jesus however knew that he had not come down to earth in order to be a miracle-worker, and certainly not to do that sort of thing merely to satisfy his own self-indulgence. That would have been a complete denial of everything he stood for, a betrayal of his very purpose in coming into the world. The stakes were high but they were not insuperable, and in resisting Satan, Jesus showed it could be done. If we resist the devil, he will flee from us, a spiritual principle Jesus demonstrated at the very outset of his earthly ministry (Jas 4:7).

Jesus' temptations were different from ours, but the way in which he responded to them carries deep lessons for us as we try to deal with this delicate subject in our own lives. First of all, he was in no doubt as to where the temptations were coming from. He knew that his enemy was Satan and did nothing to hide or obscure this fact. Today many of us are reluctant to be so blunt. Despite all the evil in the world, belief in the devil has faded away in many quarters, and talking about him and his ways is liable to get us branded as slightly crankish, even in Christian circles. This situation is ideal for Satan of course. Unlike us, the last thing he wants is recognition, because that would defeat his purpose. He works better when he is ignored, and best of all when his existence is denied. Then he can get on with the job unmolested, and if he can persuade us to attribute his activities to something else, even perhaps to God, then so much the better from his point of view.

At the present time, he is widely known in some church circles as the 'spirit', which is nothing less than a stroke of genius on his part. It is true in a way of course, because Satan is indeed a spirit, but the word is so vague that it is easily misconstrued to mean the Holy Spirit, whom to attack would be blasphemy. It is therefore possible for Satan to operate in the guise of his sworn enemy, and to persuade people to accept what he says and does because to dis-agree is to incur the charge of being 'unspiritual' and opposed to the will of God. Let us consider some examples of how this works. It is now common to hear people whose actions are a total denial of Christ dismiss criticism by saying that they were led by the 'spirit' to do things at variance with the revealed will of God in his Word. For example, people now feel led to get divorced and remarried, to live a gay lifestyle, or to let their own wishes usurp the clear commands of Scripture in some other way, and they attribute this leading to the 'spirit'. It may be hard to find anything in the Bible to support this claim, but that does not worry these people because they put the living voice of the 'spirit' above the written word of Scripture. If the two seem to conflict, as they often do, it is the living voice that wins out every time. They even have a Bible verse they use to justify this approach – 'the letter kills, but the Spirit gives life' (2 Cor. 3:6). Here we have a situation in which the devil is nowhere in sight, and yet he is in complete control! For this reason, the first lesson Jesus gives us is that we should identify our enemy and name him for who and what he is. Once that happens his power is effectively broken, because nobody is likely to follow Satan knowingly – after all, even Adam and Eve did not know who he was when they did his bidding.

So the first thing to recognize is that temptations come from Satan, who is always trying to drag us back to where we were before we came to know Christ. The second thing is to study how Jesus reacted to them and learn from that what we should do in similar circumstances. When the devil tempted him, Jesus quoted Scripture back as his answer. He knew that the Bible had been given for this purpose, to help us in times of trouble and to guide us as to how we should react. In the Scriptures we find principles laid down that are meant to guide our way of thinking in times of spiritual crisis, and it is these that enable us to answer Satan effectively. The only problem with this is that if we are to use the Word of God in this way we have to know it well enough to make it effective as our protection.

Jesus did not simply rattle off Bible texts at random. He chose his words carefully, in order to match the temptations of the devil with the right response from Scripture. For him the Bible was not a sacred object that could be quoted without regard to its meaning, but a revelation from God of his purposes for his people, which they were expected to study and apply as circumstances dictated. The Bible contains teaching that is effective when it is used properly, but to get the most out of it, we have to know what parts of it are most appropriate for dealing with the situation we are addressing. In this sense, it can be compared to a medicine chest. Every kind of medicine in it is good for something, but the skilled doctor knows which ones are right in which particular cases. This is what the expositor of Scripture is expected to know and to do. He is meant to apply the text in the most effective way and not simply assume that because it is the Word of God, it will always deliver the right result in and of itself. Today we have more copies and translations of the Bible than ever before, and yet real knowledge of the text is lower than it has been at any time since the Reformation. We should not be too surprised if unbelievers do not know what it says, but this is not the real problem. The trouble with the church today is that all too often it is believers, people who in theory honour and obey the Scriptures, whose understanding of them is woefully inadequate. Because of this, we are unable to appreciate their riches and the Bible does not speak to us as it should. The end result is that the church does not grow and is often unable to engage in the spiritual warfare to which it is called because it lacks the proper equipment for doing so successfully.

No doubt there are many reasons for this widespread ignorance today, but perhaps the most important one is that many people are unable to see that the Bible has a direct application to their lives. This is often the result of faulty teaching in the seminaries and colleges that are supposed to be training people to expound it in this way, but that concentrate on historical and critical analysis of the text at the expense of its deeper spiritual meaning and application. The result is that many sermons are more like lectures about the Bible rather than exhortations to hear and obey it, and the people whom it should be challenging never get to hear what it is really saying to them. To put this right, we have to understand that the proper use of Scripture involves three steps, which are different but related to each other, and closely interconnected in pastoral practice.

These steps are *exegesis*, *exposition* and *application*, in that order. Exegesis comes first, because unless we know what the Bible actually says and accept it as our primary authority, there is every chance that we shall not be preaching a Christian message at all. There are some preachers who expound the writings of other people – Dostoevsky perhaps or Bonhoeffer – but however Christian these writings may be, they have not been given to us for the purpose of spiritual edification and cannot take the place of the Bible in the church. Again, there are some preachers who are always talking about politics or social affairs, but even if what they say is true, they cannot be called ministers of God's Word. Within the church, it is often the case that we find two of these steps in working order, but with a debilitating weakness in the third, which undermines their effectiveness. If the weakness is in the exegesis, we shall probably end up with a situation similar to that of the Roman Catholic Church. Rome has a well-developed systematic theology and excellent pastoral application – there is an answer to every question, a solution to every problem, a place for everyone under its umbrella. But its biblical foundations are weak, to say the least. It bases its teachings on the doctrine that the apostle Peter was the first bishop of Rome and that he was given an infallible teaching authority by Jesus himself, which has been passed on to his successors. Unfortunately for them, such notions are alien to the New Testament, and the fact that the full-blown doctrine proclaimed today did not emerge until 1870 must seem somewhat suspicious. Nevertheless, that is the claim Rome makes and its historical improbability weakens the whole system.

On the other hand, if application is the weak spot, we are liable to end up with something like the conservative Lutheran, Presbyterian or Reformed churches, which have solid exegesis and excellent theology but somehow find it difficult to communicate the message to ordinary people. What they teach is often a kind of 'dead orthodoxy' that appeals to intellectuals but seldom has a much wider impact. Finally, if the missing link is exposition, what we may end up with is something like the modern evangelical church, where pastors leap from exegesis (which may be surprisingly competent) to application (which is often very practical) without passing through any discernible theological filter. The result is that they tend to disconnect immediate pastoral application from any overall principle, and therefore cut it off from its source in the biblical text. They may then find it hard to demonstrate that the advice they give fits into a coherent overall picture and so run the risk of mistaking common sense (at best) or prejudice (at worst) for God's Word to his people.

Let us now look in detail at *exegesis*, which is meant to give us an understanding of what the text actually says. Here the modern church does reasonably well, with a vast array of commentaries and study guides to tell us what the original words mean or meant in their context. Exegesis is an essential first step, because if we do not know what the Bible says, or worse, if we misinterpret it because we think we know what it means but have got it wrong, then anything we do on the basis of that will be mistaken and could turn out to be disastrous. We do not have to look very far to find examples of this. For instance, the ESV translates 1 Corinthians 2:14 as follows: 'The natural person does not accept the things of the Spirit of God.' That sounds perfectly easy to understand, and most theologically trained people will know what it means, but it is not the right translation of the original Greek. The problem is with the words 'natural person', which this version of the Bible uses to translate *psychikos anthrōpos*. *Anthrōpos* is much the easier of the two words to deal with. Traditionally, it has been translated as 'man', meaning the human race in general, but recently this has fallen out of favour in English because of the confusion between 'man' in this sense and the more restricted use of 'man' to mean 'male'. The claim has been made that to say 'natural man' as the Authorized Version does, is now unacceptably 'sexist' and must be replaced by something more generic. 'Person' is an alternative widely used in secular life, and it is clear that the translators have adopted it here for that reason. The snag is that in theology, 'person' is already used to mean something else. In the creeds, for example, we say that when the Son of God became incarnate he became a man (*anthrōpos*), but if we replace this word with 'person' we end up saying something deeply heretical. The Son of God did not become a person at his incarnation because he was a person already – the second Person of the Trinity! 'Person' is therefore not a good translation for *anthrōpos* in a theological context, and something else should be used instead. 'Human being' is probably the best translation, even though it means using two words instead of one, because it avoids the theological ambiguity inherent in 'person'.

That solution may be a bit awkward, but it is easy compared to finding a translation for *psychikos*. This is the adjective formed from the Greek word for 'soul' (*psychē*) and it has no ready equivalent in English. We can hardly say 'psychic human being' since that gives entirely the wrong impression, even though the English word 'psychic' is originally no more than an adaptation of the Greek *psychikos*. The Latin word for 'soul' is *anima*, but it would sound comic for us to say 'animal human being' and there is no telling what pictures might be conjured up in some people's imaginations. 'Soulish human being' will not do either, since English does not really have such a word. So what do we do? Probably, the only solution is to use some other word, like 'unspiritual' or perhaps even 'unregenerate', and explain the difficulty in a footnote. 'Natural' (*physikos* in Greek) is not a good option because it suggests we are talking about Adam and Eve in their original created state and not about the fallen human beings we now are. In the early church, theologians took great pains to insist that since the fall, we have been *unnatural* because our natures have been corrupted by sin. Perhaps it was true that Adam and Eve did not know the things of the Spirit of God before they fell, but if so it was for a different reason.[2] What Paul was talking about here was not the 'natural person', whatever that might mean, but the 'unregenerate human being', which is a much more precise theological term. This matters for our understanding of the biblical text, partly because it is a heresy to believe we are evil by nature and partly because Jesus was also a 'natural person', but his nature was divine and it is nonsensical to suggest he did not know the things of the Spirit of God!

Having got our exegesis right, we can move on to the second stage, which is *exposition*, and here modern preachers often fall down badly. True exposition of the Bible does not mean explaining exegetical points in individual verses (as we have just done in the preceding paragraphs), though all too often that is what it boils down to. Real exposition of an individual word or text can be done only in the light of the Scriptures as a whole. As the Reformers put it, it is essential to bear in mind 'the whole counsel of God' when preaching on any given passage or book of the Bible. To do that

---

2. They had not been given the knowledge of good and evil, so it is hard to see how they could have known the 'things of the Spirit' in the New Testament sense of the term, but arguments about this are necessarily speculative and probably ought to be avoided for that reason.

means accepting that the Bible is a coherent whole, presenting a consistent picture of one God and his plan for his people. Today, however, the analytical tendency of modern exegesis has resulted in the widespread belief that the Bible is not a single book, that it contains many different (and even contradictory) theologies and that one reason Christians are divided is that they tend to choose what suits them in Scripture and ignore anything that contradicts it. According to this way of thinking, trouble comes when one group insists that its interpretation is right and that those who disagree with it are wrong, when in fact they may just be reading some other part of the Bible that supports their way of thinking equally well. The only answer, say these people, is to accept that the Bible often cannot be made to say one thing over against another, and so the church must be tolerant and accept the coexistence of contradictory theologies in its midst. You read it one way and I read it another way, goes the argument, but we are both sincere and equally right in claiming that our opinions are the Word of God, even if they do not tie up with one another. Some people even argue that what we are dealing with here is the famous Hegelian opposition between the 'thesis' and its 'antithesis', which will one day give rise to a higher and more satisfactory 'synthesis', when sides that oppose each other now will discover a common solution in a transformed intellectual atmosphere. The snag with this is that God did not consult Hegel when he revealed his Word to his people. If there is a 'thesis' as opposed to an 'antithesis' in Scripture, it is the opposition between belief and unbelief, and no 'synthesis' of these two things will ever be possible. Indeed, one could write the history of ancient Israel as a failed attempt to find such a synthesis (more properly known as 'syncretism'), which was roundly condemned and rejected by a long line of prophets, whose words now form a substantial part of the sacred text.

It is because this approach has gained such widespread currency that we find biblical interpretation in chaos in the church today. Unlikely and even impossible theories are espoused on the basis of individual verses with little or no attention being paid to the overall thrust of the whole. So common is this tendency nowadays that many biblical scholars dislike the very notion of theology and refuse to let it intrude on their exegetical work. Only recently a prominent biblical scholar told me in all seriousness that although he understood the Bible, he could never get his mind around Christian doctrine! It is now fairly common to find study guides that outline the approach and emphases of particular books, but with little connection made to the whole of the Bible. Instead of the eternal message of God, we are presented with the circumstantial reactions of the apostle Paul, of one of the Evangelists or perhaps of some anonymous writer of the second generation of Christians who was passing himself off as an apostle. In this climate, it is no wonder that the message of the text is obscured and the Bible becomes almost impossible to use effectively for devotional or pastoral purposes. As a popular expression puts it, we cannot see the wood for the trees.

To use the Bible effectively we must recognize that it is a book inspired by God and that it talks primarily about him. In the final analysis, God's revelation is self-revelation – in it, he is speaking to us about himself and opening up his mind to us. It is nonsense to claim that it is possible to read the Bible without theology, because that is ultimately what the Bible is all about. Failure to realize this says only that we have not grasped the meaning of the text and are therefore unable to make use of it effectively. Indeed, any attempt we might make to put the Scriptures into practice is liable to go badly wrong unless our theology is sorted out; it is rather like taking medicine without reading the instructions first! Only when we have understood that can we move on to the third aspect of biblical interpretation, which is *application*. This is where the answers of Jesus to Satan come in. Given who it was he was talking to, Jesus did not have to lay the groundwork of exegesis and exposition, since Satan knew those things already. But application was another matter. It could not be taken as read because each situation demands a fresh approach. Commentaries and theological textbooks may enjoy a long life, but sermons have to be geared to the audience at hand, even if the principles they contain are of universal value. There is no getting around this; Jesus joined battle with the devil not by explaining Scripture, nor by expounding its meaning, but by applying it to the circumstances at hand, and we must also learn to do this if we are to fight the spiritual battles to which we have been called.

Today we are in desperate need of a living preaching and teaching ministry that can recapture the pastoral use of Scripture and set us back on the road to proper spiritual development. If you do not believe this, ask most people today what it means to them to be 'filled with the Spirit' (Eph. 5:18). How many are likely to respond that it means being filled with a knowledge of the Word of God? The chances are that you will be told that to be filled with the Spirit means doing strange things that ordinary people are incapable of and that make little sense to the uninitiated. Today, a 'Spirit-filled person' is liable to be thought of as someone who speaks in tongues, has visions, gets so-called 'words of knowledge' or even falls down on the floor and starts barking like a dog. Such a person may also be capable of preaching an inspiring message that warms the hearts of those who hear him and sets them on fire for the Lord, but this will not be his defining characteristic. Sadly, we must admit that many of those who see the faults with this approach react against it by going to the opposite extreme and sending their hearers to sleep with erudite but irrelevant homilies. A few even quote Greek and Hebrew words in their sermons, a practice that does nothing other than convince the average churchgoer that their preacher lives on another planet – something that some of them probably suspected already. Others believe that they have to lighten their message with humour, whether it is relevant or not, and contribute to the widespread notion that preaching, and indeed worship in general, is largely a form of entertainment. Jesus teaches us that Scripture is a weapon of our warfare against the forces of Satan, a two-edged sword that pierces to the dividing line between soul and spirit, between the things of this world and the things of the world above. Used properly, it is the most powerful weapon we have. If we study it diligently and apply it correctly we shall resist the temptations that come up against us and then the prayer of Jesus will be fulfilled. If we abuse it, we may succeed in fooling ourselves for a while, but in the end our folly will catch up with us and the latter state will be much worse than the first.

But deliver us from evil

It is one thing to learn how to resist temptation, but quite another to be delivered from evil. The two things are related of course – temptation comes from the devil and the devil is the prince of evil. But even if we manage not to be led into temptation, it does not automatically follow that we shall be delivered from evil as well. One of the reasons for this is that temptation is the gateway only to certain kinds of evil; there are other kinds that do not necessarily attack us by that means but from which we also need deliverance. Another reason is that evil is ever-present in our lives as long as we are in this world, whether we feel the force of temptation or not. As the Lord's Prayer indicates by the words it uses, *temptation* is something we are led into, but *evil* is something we have to be led out of. Our relationship to it is fundamentally different, and so we have to consider evil as a problem in its own right and not merely as something that affects us if we have the misfortune to succumb to temptation.

What is evil? This question has dominated a good deal of theological discussion ever since the early days of the Christian church. The Bible teaches that the world was created by a God who is good, omnipresent and omnipotent, and that everything in it is essentially good (Gen. 1:31). Logically, therefore, evil should not exist at all because there is no room for it in such a universe. But as a matter of fact, everyone agrees that there is such a thing as 'evil' in the world, even if there are arguments about how it should be defined. Christians have therefore had to face the question of how evil can exist and be as powerful as it is in a universe controlled by a God whose goodness is incompatible with it. Theologians call this problem 'theodicy' ('divine judgment') and, despite many attempts, none of them has ever managed to produce a fully convincing answer to it. Nevertheless, there are some things we can say about it that will help us to understand what the parameters of the discussion are, even if they cannot solve all our problems. We can outline these parameters as follows.

1. *The world was created by a good God who remains in control of it.* Whatever evil is and however it manifests itself, it cannot be blamed on him.

2. *Evil exists and is felt as such by human beings, whether they are Christians or not.* Indeed, one of the strongest arguments against

the truth of Christianity is the existence of evil. How can a God of love allow this if he is really who he says he is?

3. *Natural phenomena are not evil.* This is perhaps a more contentious proposition, and there are certainly some people who have said that natural phenomena can be evil, but a little reflection will show that this argument does not stand up to serious investigation. By 'natural phenomena' we mean things like earthquakes and volcanic eruptions, but also including famines and epidemics of various kinds. As far as earthquakes and the like are concerned, the notion that they are somehow evil probably goes back to the great Lisbon earthquake of 1755, which killed thousands of people and destroyed one of the great cities of Europe. That made a great impact on contemporaries, who found it hard to believe that a Christian nation, in which the church prayed every day for the safety and protection of its people, could have been subjected to such a terrible scourge. Since then, of course, our knowledge and experience of such things has greatly increased and now it is virtually impossible for a disaster of that kind to strike without the entire world being alerted to it. In 2004, a tsunami killed thousands of people in the countries surrounding the Indian Ocean, but although everyone agrees that this was a great tragedy, can we really say that it was 'evil'? All over the world people are dying of starvation caused by famine and of diseases spread by mysterious viruses, for which there is no known cure. Again, these are tragedies, but is it right to use the word 'evil' to describe them?

The main reason for my hesitation about saying this is that there is nothing in these phenomena themselves that can be ascribed to malicious intent. Earthquakes do not set out to kill people deliberately, and geologists know perfectly well that they are part of an ongoing development and reshaping of the earth's surface. We all know that there is one pending in California and that when it comes, it will be a major disaster for those living there at the time, but we also know that very few people take that as a reason to move away. When the disaster strikes, there will be any number of commentators who will blame its effects on God and probably quite a few people will lose their faith in the process, but is this fair? The people who live there know what is coming and have decided to risk the consequences, so what right have they got to complain? Similarly, viruses are not intentionally evil; from their point of view, they are doing no more than going through their normal life cycle in someone else's body. Unpleasant though the consequences of this may be for the poor person whose body it is, we can hardly blame the virus. In the wider perspective of reality, it may well be fulfilling a function in God's universe that is perfectly valid in its own right; it is merely unfortunate that some human beings have got in the way of what (on its own terms) is a perfectly natural development.

As understood by Christians, evil is a spiritual force opposed to the will of God. Whatever this force is, it must have been created by God originally, since nothing can exist apart from him. If that is the case, it must also have been good to start off with, since God did not create anything that was not good. Therefore, the only way the spiritual force that is now evil could have become so was by rebelling against God. For this to be possible, the force in question must be what we call 'personal', since rebellion is a personal act. The Bible portrays evil in terms of spiritual agents created with the power to rebel against God, who in fact did so, and who, because they are immortal by nature, continue to exist in the world God created.[3] The question we cannot answer is why this should have happened. The spirits who revolted against God must have known that they could never succeed, so why did they do it? Perhaps the only satisfactory answer to this is that they wanted what we call 'freedom'. Freedom is taken for granted by those who are used to it, as we in the Western world mostly are, and so it is difficult for us to appreciate the force of this argument. But for

---

3. The Greek text of the Lord's Prayer does not make it clear whether 'evil' is a thing or a personal force. The words *apo tou ponērou* can be interpreted as either neuter (referring to 'evil' as a thing) or as masculine (referring to a personal being). Most interpreters prefer the former reading, which seems to be more natural, but this does not exclude the personal character of evil. The thing would not exist without the personal agent who brought it into being.

centuries people who have been enslaved or conquered have rebelled against their fate, even when they knew perfectly well that they had no chance of succeeding. So strong has this desire for 'freedom' been that it has sometimes defied all logic. The Americans who revolted against Britain in 1776 were not oppressed by any objective criterion of oppression; in fact, they generally lived better and freer lives than most people in the British Isles at the time. Yet in spite of this self-evident truth, they managed to persuade themselves that they were slaves of an evil empire and that they were fighting for 'freedom'. Their success has enshrined this interpretation in subsequent history and legend, so that it is now embraced even by blacks and native Americans, who certainly were not freed in any meaningful sense at the time.

Similarly, Satan was not oppressed in heaven, but perhaps he felt that he was because he could not do exactly as he pleased, and once he was able to persuade enough of his fellow-angels that they were suffering under God's rule, rebellion broke out. It would be too much to say that he won, but to some extent he certainly got away with it, because God allowed him to go on existing in a kingdom of his own, even though he is not a fully independent, sovereign power. Why God should have permitted this is another mystery we cannot solve, although we have to live with the consequences and deal with them accordingly.

Satan is the evil we face, and it is from him that we must be delivered. We are told in Scripture that he goes about like a prowling lion, seeking whom he may devour (1 Pet. 5:8), and this must be our starting point in learning how to resist him. We are never safe from his attacks, and it is often when we think we are that we are in the greatest danger of all. As the prince of this world, he uses the weapons of this world in order to insinuate himself into our hearts and minds. A couple of generations ago there were tendencies in the Christian community to avoid the newly invented cinema because it was thought to be a purveyor of vice. Looking back on the silent films of the 1920s that provoked so much righteous indignation we can hardly believe it. Since then our minds have become so coarsened by a daily diet of filth purveyed to us in the media that we scarcely recognize it any more. Christians who would never buy a pornographic magazine are happy to sit, night after night, in front of the box and be entertained, if that is the word, by a steady stream of evil. Admittedly, this evil is not always shown in a positive light, and the good guys usually win out in the end, but how many of us are used to seeing television violence in real life? A friend of mine who works for the Metropolitan Police in London tells me that one of their biggest problems is with potential recruits who picture police life as an endless series of high-speed car chases through the back streets of the city, with some damsel in distress as their reward for sorting out the baddies. The fact that most of them will be behind a desk filling out boring reports only dawns on them later, after they have signed up and realize that the glamour is mainly on television, not in real life. This is no doubt a good thing, but the fact remains that it was the thrill of violence and evil that attracted them to the police force in the first place.

Purveyors of entertainment have long known that evil is more attractive than goodness. Readers of Dante's *Divine Comedy* usually agree that the cantos set in hell are the best ones, while those set in heaven are rather lacklustre by comparison. Few people would doubt that in John Milton's *Paradise Lost*, Satan is a more memorable character than God is. This is not meant to be a criticism of Dante or Milton, neither of whom approved of the evil they described, but a reminder to us that the human mind is attracted to such things however much it may protest the contrary. In the modern world, stage and screen writers wage a constant battle against anything they regard as censorship, because they know that their success depends on being able to entice us with the delectable details of evil. The invention of television has turned this age-old tendency into a cultural plague. Television viewers now have a steady diet of sex and bad language to contend with, and even news programmes tend to be full of the spicier details of prominent people's private lives. We sit there and tut-tut our disapproval, but all the while we are being gradually inured to such things and are no longer shocked when we see them before our eyes. We become bored with run-of-the-mill evil and want something ever more horrific. We may tell ourselves that it is all a fantasy, but it is a fantasy that exerts a strong appeal on our fleshly natures and makes it even harder to focus our minds on the things of God, which seem so bland and boring by comparison. The terrible truth is that we shall not turn away from evil voluntarily, because we are bored with it; we can escape only by being delivered from it, because it is in our fallen human natures to be attracted by it, however much we may know and acknowledge the harm it causes.

Evil also comes to us in the form of projects to change society. This is a complex question and there are many sides to it, but let us look at a few representative examples. Today there is a widespread belief that people should be free to do what they want, as long as they do not harm others in the process. The result is that in many places it is no longer safe for decent people to walk the streets, particularly at night. The racks at the newsagents are filled with pornography, much of it masquerading as photography, fitness or women's magazines, and it is almost impossible to avoid. Advertisements are often deliberately designed to appeal to our baser instincts, because those who produce them know only too well that this is the best way for them to sell their goods. The lives of the rich and famous are paraded in front of us, no matter how immoral they may be – indeed, the worse they are, the more we seem to want to read about them. Even legitimate news stories suffer from this bias. People who follow wars in distant places are seldom interested in the relief work being carried out by international aid agencies like the Red Cross; what they want to see are bombed-out villages, tortured prisoners and enemy leaders captured and shot on the spot. It may not be quite the same thing as throwing Christians to the lions in the arenas of ancient Rome, but the lust for the sight of blood has scarcely diminished over the years.

Evil can also take very subtle forms, even to the extent that it can parade as doing good. Go to any hot spot around the globe and there you will find hundreds of people who are living off the sufferings of those whom they are supposed to be helping. Camps are set up to house the foreign aid workers in relative comfort, because they cannot be expected to share local conditions. This in turn encourages the local elite, who act as go-betweens for the aid agencies, to opt into their lifestyle, with the result that much of the relief money that is supposed to be going to help the needy ends

up in the pockets of the resident administrators and their associ-
ates. These people need to make sure that the aid money keeps
flowing their way, because that is their only source of income, and
so they have no incentive whatsoever to improve the conditions
that caused the aid to be given in the first place. In some extreme
cases, they can even be accused of fomenting discord, or of
keeping an existing crisis going, in order not to lose the revenue
from international donors that relief aid brings. The intentions of
the original donors are good, of course, and the sentiments on
which fundraisers rely for disaster relief are noble, but all too
often the results are catastrophic. In these worst cases, only a tiny
proportion of the money raised for such causes ever reaches its
destination, and most of those who are suffering are no better off
now than they were before. Here indeed is evil masquerading as
good, and doing so with such effectiveness that it is often almost
impossible to criticize it.

Nor is this all. The public's supposed right to know, a device
meant to protect us from the machinations of impersonal government, has produced situations in which registered paedophiles
have been identified to their neighbours, with consequences too
frightening to contemplate. Recently, a case in England occurred
after the serial killing of five prostitutes. An intensive police investigation turned up a likely suspect, who subsequently had to be
released because another more promising candidate had been
found and the evidence that had led to the first man's arrest turned
out to be flimsy. Of course, the man originally arrested was not a
lily-white innocent. He had known the girls in question quite well
because he had been one of their regular customers. One could
easily argue that anyone in that position must expect to suffer the
consequences if things turn out badly. However, not only was the
man arrested and questioned for several days; his name, address,
occupation and other details were flashed across the television
screens of the entire country on the assumption that he was guilty
and would not be returning to private life. When he was released
after a few days in custody, he discovered that his life had been
destroyed by the ever-intrusive media, which had tried, condemned and virtually executed him merely in order to satisfy what
they perceived as public demand. What motivated the reporters

was the public's desire to know what was going on. But at what point does the public's right to know become an intolerable invasion of privacy and the source of ultimate injustice? Do we really need to know all the gory details of the lives of people who are of no immediate concern to us? What does this do for those who have been convicted but who have subsequently repented of their crime and are trying to leave their past behind them, but who cannot do so because the entire neighbourhood is publicly informed of it? Is any public interest served by this kind of thing?

'Deliver us from evil.' Outward evils are terrible things but they pale into insignificance when we are attacked from within. Temptation may be unpleasant, but at least it comes from outside ourselves and can be resisted with the right spiritual treatment. Chronic depression does not go away so easily. Many people are haunted by inner torments they do not understand and cannot control. A wide range of possible causes, both physical and mental, can be identified but it is fiendishly difficult to cure them and those so afflicted may be driven to suicide in despair at ever being released from their torment. What can we do about this? Obviously, we must go on looking for cures as much as we can, but that is of very limited help in dealing with the cases we come across on a day-to-day basis. We can pray for them and try to encourage them to trust in God for deliverance, but we have to accept that there will be times when there is nothing we can do. God knows those who are his and we must trust him even when we have no human comfort to offer. Knowing our limitations is far better than pretending that we do not have any, and that we can solve every problem if only we persist. Some things are beyond our understanding, and when we come up against them, we must simply trust in God who can do things of which we can only dream.

We may also experience evil as the innocent victims of other people's folly. What can we say to those who are maimed for life because some drunken driver swerved off the road just as they were coming along it in the wrong direction? What good does it do to reflect that adequate car insurance should be compulsory, when a teenager who has stolen a vehicle to go on a joyride ends up killing himself and others in his immature stupidity? Ultimately, we have no defence against such things, and the newspapers remind us that they happen somewhere to someone almost every day. 'Deliver us from evil.' It is a prayer that has many dimensions to it, not least the fear of sudden death or injury caused by the antisocial behaviour of irresponsible people over whom we have no control.

At the end of the day, evil is a spiritual force that can be defeated only on the spiritual level. As long as we live in this world we shall be exposed to it one way or another, and often it will come to us in several different ways at the same time. In our fallen world a web of perverted logic lumps together the supremely good with the supremely evil and condemns them both together. Recently, a highly effective programme for the redemption of prisoners, called Inner Change, was banned from British prisons because it was supposed to be the work of 'fundamentalists', and as any newspaper reporter will tell you, a fundamentalist is somebody who drives planes into skyscrapers on a suicide mission that achieves nothing beyond the deaths of thousands of innocent people. Many otherwise rational souls have no problem in linking these two things together as part of the same phenomenon of religious extremism, which they regard as highly dangerous. Logically so, from their point of view, because in a world where everything is relative, those who are prepared to die for their beliefs pose a real threat to the established order. Evangelical Christians have little in common with the Taliban, but on this point they are at one, and are perceived as such by those who do not share their outlook. To the liberal minds of our time, 'deliver us from evil' means 'deliver us from fanaticism of any kind'. As Bishop Joseph Butler said to John Wesley, whose evangelistic fervour he deplored, 'Enthusiasm, sir, is a very horrid thing.' There is no getting around the fact that evangelical Christians are enthusiastic and sincere about their beliefs, and we must very much hope that we would also be prepared to die for them if necessary. The irony is that at one level this puts us on a par with a man like Adolf Hitler, who was also enthusiastic and sincere, and who may be said to have died for his beliefs. Our critics think they see a common thread here and may even call us neo-Nazis, but how fair an assessment is this?

The evil we associate with Hitler and the Taliban is a spiritual force that cannot be defeated by the conventional weapons of secular warfare, however hard we may try. If secularists think that evangelical Christians resemble these monsters in some way, it is because we appreciate that the struggle we are engaged in is a spiritual one. This is a dimension that completely escapes the secular mind, which rejects the existence of anything spiritual, whether it is good or bad. In praying for deliverance from evil, we are not praying, as the secularists would wish, to be set free from spiritual things, but for the triumph of good spiritual forces over evil ones. Here there is a gap in comprehension that reflects the abyss which separates those who believe in Christ from those who do not. It is pointless to argue with those who claim that there is no God merely because they have not found him at the end of a telescope or in the laboratory. God is not a material object who can be examined by the techniques of natural science, and those who are limited to that will never find him. What we believe is that the material world is not all there is, because the great questions of life lie beyond it.

Good and evil are not to be found in physical things, but they exist, and each of them claims our allegiance. Those who are born into the world are born into the kingdom of Satan and are subject to evil, whether they want to be or not. The scientific atheist is no different from anyone else in this respect, and his blindness to this reality is only further proof of the power it has to hold human beings in its grip. In the twentieth century, professed atheists and their systems wreaked more havoc and killed more innocent people than all the religious fanatics in history put together. If ever there was an ideology that stands discredited by its results, this is it. Yet atheists continue to claim that they are the harbingers of enlightenment and not the accomplices of death, and a world that does not want to face up to the claims of God is only too willing to listen to their siren voices. Goodness does not come naturally to people who are trapped in a fallen world. We cannot work our way out of evil; we must be delivered from it. Many agencies in the world are trying to do what is good and to put right the chaos and disorder they see around them. Very often, these organizations are run by altruistic people whose dedication to their cause puts most

Christians to shame. Yet we know that in spite of all their efforts, they are doomed to fail in the end because they have not grasped what the root of the trouble is. As Christians, our warfare is on a different plane to theirs and to them it is both incomprehensible and frightening, but, at the same time, it is the only strategy that will win in the end. In this we have the promise of Christ, who has made us part of his church, against which the gates of hell will not prevail (Matt. 16:18). This is our assurance; this is our hope. In the end, God will vindicate his people and deliver us from evil, so that we may reign with him in his glory, world without end. Amen.

6. FOR YOURS IS THE KINGDOM AND THE POWER AND THE GLORY, FOR EVER. AMEN

And so we come to the end of the Lord's Prayer. The familiar coda that usually accompanies its public recitation today was not part of the original text, and the best guess is that it was added at a fairly late stage in the transmission of Matthew's Gospel. It was not in the fourth-century manuscripts used by Jerome to translate the New Testament into Latin and so it formed no part of the prayer for most of the Western Middle Ages. It was added by the Protestant reformers, mainly because of Erasmus, the great humanist scholar who edited the Greek New Testament and retranslated it into Latin in 1516. Erasmus found it in the Greek manuscripts he had in front of him, and assumed that because Greek was the original language of the New Testament, those manuscripts must be right and the Latin translation defective. He had no idea it was the Greek manuscripts that had been embellished over time, because he had no access to Greek texts that dated from the time of Jerome. Since the sixteenth century, our knowledge has increased enormously and we now have plenty of Greek manuscript evidence to prove that it was Jerome and not Erasmus who had the better text. Nevertheless, the Lord's Prayer

seems somehow incomplete without the final doxology, and there
is evidence that it was already being added in apostolic times. This
evidence comes from the *Didache*, an anonymous work of the late
first (or possibly early second) century, where the Lord's Prayer is
written out in full and this doxology is added, though without any
reference to the kingdom (*Didache* 8.2).[1] Because of this, the additional words are usually retained in public worship, which is where
most of us encounter the Prayer on a regular basis, and so I shall
say something about them by way of conclusion.

The purpose and effect of the doxology is to bring us back to
the beginning, to round off our prayer and wrap it up with the
reminder that everything comes from God and returns to him.
To him belongs the kingdom, the power and the glory, for ever
and ever. As found in the *Didache*, the doxology has only two elements – the power and the glory. The first of these speaks of what
God does and the second of who God is, a pairing that is normal
in ancient texts, though logically it should be the other way round,
since what God does depends on who he is. However, there is Old
Testament precedent for this order, which is found in David's
prayer recorded in 1 Chronicles 29:11. The same combination
appears in Psalm 63:2, in a slightly expanded form in Daniel 2:37
and then in Matthew 24:30 (paralleled in Mark 13:26 and Luke
21:27). Interestingly, it is only in the book of Revelation, the most
purely 'theological' book in the New Testament, that we find the
words in their logical order (4:11; 15:8; 19:1). It is the addition of
the word 'kingdom' that is later, though it probably derives from 1
Chronicles 29:11 also. There, the expression is 'greatness, power
and glory', but the word 'kingdom' appears in the next line and it
would have been a simple matter to elide it into the doxology at
the end of the Lord's Prayer.

Mention of the kingdom recalls the second line of the prayer,
but it also provides the context for the power and the glory, which
are best understood as aspects of the kingdom. It was common in
ancient rhetoric to express things in threes, and usually the second
and third elements in the trilogy were added to reinforce the

---

1. The text is very similar to the Matthaean version of the Prayer.

meaning of the first.[2] If that is the case here, then 'power' expresses what the kingdom does and 'glory' emphasizes what the kingdom is. In the kingdom of God, function and status belong together and are equally supreme. There is no power apart from God's power, and no glory apart from his glory either. Furthermore, his kingdom is an eternal one. It had no beginning and will have no end. Its power does not fluctuate in the way that the power of an earthly kingdom does; it does not go through periods of growth and decline in the way that human institutions do. It is simply there.

Jesus came into a world in which the might of Rome could not be challenged, and in which the Jewish people continued to offer the sacrifices in the temple that had been prescribed by Moses and had carried on with only short interruptions since the time of Solomon. Within a generation of his death and resurrection, that Jewish world would be swept away for ever, and not even the modern state of Israel has been able (or willing) to restore it. Rome would last a good deal longer, but in the end its power and glory would vanish into the sands of history too, ironically leaving behind the church as its most enduring legatee. Today it seems to many that the age of European-dominated Christianity is coming to an end. Already, the bulk of the church's membership is to be found in the non-Western world, and many of the traditionally Christian countries of Europe and America seem determined to turn their backs on their heritage. The world is changing, and the church of the future will look very different from anything we have known hitherto.

But whatever happens in the years ahead, one thing remains certain. The kingdom of God will not change. Its power and glory will be as visible then as they are now, in the lives of changed men and women who have taken up their cross and followed Jesus. The words of the Lord's Prayer, and the theology it proclaims, will remain embedded in the hearts and minds of believers long after the current challenges we face have disappeared. Our Father

---

2. Though not always. In 1 Cor. 13:13 ('faith, hope and love') it is the other way round.

remains on his throne in heaven, from whence his kingdom will one day surely come to embrace us all. May he hasten that day when we shall be gathered for ever around his throne and our prayers on earth will be merged with the glorious song of victory of the Lamb who is seated upon it and who makes intercession for us, world without end, amen.

APPENDIX: THE TWO VERSIONS OF THE LORD'S PRAYER

The text of Matthew (6:9–13) is given below, with the shorter Lucan version in italic type.

Our *Father* in heaven,
  hallowed be your name.
Your kingdom come,
  your will be done,
  on earth as it is in heaven.
Give us this[1] day our daily bread,
and forgive us our debts,[2]
  as we also have forgiven our debtors.
And lead us not into temptation,
  but deliver us from evil.

[For yours is the kingdom and the power and the glory, for ever. Amen.]

---

1. Luke's version has 'each'.
2. Luke's version has 'sins'.

For this study, I have modified the above text in the fourth petition, to read, 'Forgive us our sins, as we forgive those who sin against us.' That translation is often found in modern liturgical texts.

SCRIPTURE INDEX